HOW TO PREPARE EFFECTIVE MESSAGES

G. Michael Cocoris

© 2010 by G. Michael Cocoris

All rights reserved. This publication may not be reproduced (in whole or in part, edited, or revised) in any way, form, or means, including, but not limited to electronic, mechanical, photocopying, recording or any kind of storage and retrieval system *for sale*, except for brief quotations in printed reviews, without the written permission of G. Michael Cocoris, 2016 Euclid #20, Santa Monica, CA 90405, michaelcocoris@gmail.com, his appointed representatives. Permission is hereby granted, however, for the reproduction of the whole or parts of the whole without changing the content in any way for *free distribution*, provided all copies contain this copyright notice in its entirety. Permission is also granted to charge for the cost of copying.

Unless otherwise indicated, all Scripture quotations are taken from the New King James Version ®, Copyright © 1979, 1980, 1982 by Thomas Nelson, Inc. Used by permission. All rights reserved.

TABLE OF CONTENTS

Preface

Chapter

1	Introduction: Preach The Word	1
2	Messages That Preach The Word	7
3	Messages That Are Properly Prepared	13
4	Messages That Are Effective	21
5	Messages That Are Clear	33
6	Messages That People Can Follow	39
7	Messages That Keep People's Attention	45
8	Messages That Move People's Feet	55
9	Messages That Grab People By The Ears	63
10	Messages That Attract People	75
11	Messages That Pack A Punch	81
12	Messages That Are Appealing	89
13	Conclusion	93

Appendix: Peter's Sermon In Acts 2   97

Bibliography   105

About The Author   107

PREFACE

Everyone who has spoken publicly wrestles with how to put together a clear, effective, and interesting presentation. We have heard others communicate effectively. You may have done it yourself. Then, there are those times when you have felt that someone, or maybe even you, delivered an unclear, ineffective, or uninteresting message. At those moments, you ask yourself, "How can I prepare effective messages?" I have asked that question many times over the course of many years. As a young man, I felt deeply that I had something to say and I wanted to say it as effectively as possible. I began wrestling with the question of how to do that.

In college, I took a basic speech course. The textbook was the classic *Principles and Types of Speech* by Allan H. Monroe. That course was helpful. During those years, I also spoke and learned from my mistakes.

In seminary, I had the privilege of having Dr. Haddon Robinson as a homiletics professor (homiletics is the science and art of preaching). Dr. Robinson is the author of *Biblical Preaching*. I highly recommend that you read his book. He is now recognized as one of the leading homileticians in the country. His teaching has shaped my speaking. As will be evident, a great deal of what he taught me is reflected in the following pages.

As an adjunct professor, I taught evangelism for five years at Dallas Seminary. I also worked under Dr. Robinson in the homiletics department during that time, listening to and evaluating sermons. That experience further ingrained in me Dr. Robinson's concepts. With what Dr. Robinson taught me as a foundation and framework, along with my own experience of preaching and teaching for over fifty years, I have reached some conclusions concerning what constitutes a clear, effective, and interesting message. What follows are my conclusions. They apply to preaching and to teaching the Bible.

A speech contains a title, an introduction, a subject, an outline, material to support the various points in the outline, and a conclusion. All of these and more will be discussed, but not in that order. The order of this presentation is the order a speaker should use in *preparing* a message. Therefore, the introduction and the title will be dealt with last, because, as a rule (there are exceptions), the introduction should be prepared after the other parts of the speech have been put together. After all, how do you know what you need to introduce until you have figured out what you are going to say?

What follows is a discussion of what makes an effective message and the procedure to develop one. It focuses on the method of preparing a message, but it should be kept in mind that, as Bishop William A. Quayle said, preaching is *not* the art of making and delivering a sermon. "Preaching is the art of making a preacher and delivering that" (Robinson, p. 24).

I wish to thank Teresa Rogers for proofreading this material. I trust that this material and this procedure will enable you to produce clearer, more effective, and more interesting messages in less time.

G.. Michael Cocoris
Santa Monica, CA

Chapter 1
Introduction: Preach The Word

Preaching or teaching the Bible is speaking in public, but it differs from public speaking. The distinctive element of preaching/teaching the Bible is the content of the message. By its very nature, preaching/teaching the Bible demands that the message be a biblical message.

God solemnly charges, "Preach the word" (2 Tim. 4:2). The context of that command indicates that no matter how far people are from God and His Word, the messenger of God is to *proclaim* the *Word of God*. Notice what Paul writes to Timothy. It applies to today's situation.

Difficult Days Paul began by saying, "In the last days perilous times will come" (2 Tim. 3:1). The Greek word translated "perilous" means "hard to deal with, difficult, hard to bear, painful, grievous." He then described such a time in detail. "For men will be lovers of themselves, lovers of money, boasters, proud, blasphemers, disobedient to parents, unthankful, unholy, unloving, unforgiving, slanderers, without self-control, brutal, despisers of good, traitors, headstrong, haughty, lovers of pleasure rather than lovers of God, having a form of godliness but denying its power. And from such people turn away!" (2 Tim. 3:2-5).

Preach the Word After making some other comments, Paul tells Timothy what to do. He writes, "But you must continue in the things which you have learned and been assured of, knowing from whom you have learned *them,* and that from childhood you have known the Holy Scriptures, which are able to make you wise for salvation through faith which is in Christ Jesus. All Scripture *is* given by inspiration of God and *is* profitable for doctrine, for reproof, for correction, for instruction in righteousness, that the man of God may be complete, thoroughly equipped for every good work. I charge *you,* therefore, before God and the Lord Jesus Christ, who will judge the living and the dead at His appearing and His kingdom: Preach the word! Be ready in season *and* out of season. Convince, rebuke, exhort, with all longsuffering and teaching" (2 Tim 3:14-4:2).

Paul predicted that difficult days would come. I submit to you that they are here. What are we to do? Paul's answer is that we have a Word from God and we are to *preach the Word*!

Preach

Paul says, "Preach the Word." The Greek word for "preach" means "to be a herald, to proclaim." Pointing out that it was the word for a herald's proclamation from a king, Barclay says it implies specific characteristics, such as 1) Source. The message is from the king, a source from beyond the messenger. It is not the personal opinion of the messenger. 2) Authority. The announcement was "the king's law, the king's command, and the king's decision." 3) Certainty (no, perhaps, maybe, or probably). Goethe says, "Tell me of your certainties: I have doubts enough of my own." Preaching is the proclamation of certainties, and a man cannot make others sure of that about which he himself is in doubt (Barclay on Matthew 3).

Introduction: Preach The Word

The Word

Paul says, "Preach the *Word*." The *message* of the speech (sermon, lesson) must be a *message* from the Word.

The Misuse of the Word Virtually all preachers claim they are preaching the Word, but obviously, not all are doing that. Many misuse the Word.

Some use the text as a pretext to proclaim their own ideas. They read a biblical text at the beginning of their message and never refer to it again. Robinson suggests, "It is like playing the national anthem at a football game. It gets things started and is never heard from again throughout the game" (Robinson, p. 20).

Others jump from text to text, with the result that their message, that is, not exactly what the Word of God is saying. The text only serves as a "proof-text" for the speaker's ideas. Thus, the speaker's message is not the text's message. It is the message of the speaker, who is using the words of the text but with a meaning that is different from the original author.

The Proper Handling of the Word In the final analysis, preaching God's Word *explains* (applies, etc.) what *God* says. Such proclamation is "expository preaching." That expression is often misunderstood. The concept of expository preaching is clarified in the next chapter.

Exposition puts the Scripture at the center of the public ministry. It forces the speaker to stay within the context of the passage. When done properly, it speaks to the situation of the day. It releases the power of the Word of God among the people of God.

Many have applauded expository preaching as the best of all preaching. In their book *Variety in Your Preaching*, Whitesell and

Perry say, "Most homileticians and preachers will award first place to this type of preaching (Expository Method) as the most desirable since it adheres more closely to the apostolic pattern, honors the Word more, and establishes people more firmly in the knowledge of the Word" (Whitesell and Perry, p. 34).

When he resigned from his church, a pastor gave his people advice on selecting his successor, which directly shows the necessity for an expository ministry. "Do not choose a man who always preaches on isolated texts; I care not how powerful and eloquent he may be. The effect of his eloquence will be to banish a taste for the Word of God and substitute a taste for the preacher in its place" (Ramm, p. 97, quoting *Moody Monthly*).

The Reason

Those who speak for God must publicly broadcast *God's* message because God uses the public proclamation of His message to change people spiritually. God saves and sanctifies people through the preaching of His Word.

Saves Paul says, "For this reason, we also thank God without ceasing because when you received the word of God which you heard from us, you welcomed it not as the word of men, but as it is in truth, the word of God, which also effectively works in you who believe" (1 Thess. 2:13). In this passage, the expression the "Word of God" refers to the gospel. When Paul preached the gospel to the Thessalonians, they welcomed it; they believed it was a message from God, not a message of human origin. Consequently, it effectively worked in them. The phrase "effectively works" is all one word in Greek and means "to be at work, to be in action, to operate." God works through the preaching of *His* message.

Introduction: Preach The Word

God Himself speaks through the personality and message of a preacher to confront men and women and bring them to Himself (Robinson, p. 18).

Peter says something similar. He says, "Having been born again, not of corruptible seed but incorruptible, through the word of God which lives and abides forever" (1 Pet. 1:23) and a few verses later adds, "Now this is the word which by the gospel was preached to you" (1 Pet. 1:25). The original recipients of Peter's letter were born again through the preaching of the Word of God.

Sanctifies Paul says to the Romans, "For I long to see you, that I may impart to you some spiritual gift, so that you may be established" (Rom. 1:11). By imparting some spiritual gift to them, he does not mean that he would bestow spiritual gifts such as teaching or exhortation. Instead, he means that he would exercise his spiritual gift and, in so doing, bless and benefit them. The spiritual blessings that they would receive would be a gift. Paul desired to be personally present with them so that he might benefit them spiritually. Not even the inspired letter of Romans could substitute for it. In other words, the preaching/teaching ministry of Paul would establish them in the faith, even after they had received the book of Romans! (Gal. 4:20).

Paul writes that Scripture is "profitable for doctrine, for reproof, for correction, for instruction in righteousness, that the man of God may be complete, thoroughly equipped for every good work" (2 Tim. 3:16-17). Therefore, those who speak for God must "preach the word." They must "be ready in season *and* out of season. Convince, rebuke, exhort, with all longsuffering and teaching" (2 Tim. 4:2).

Note, the Scripture is profitable for doctrine and instruction in righteousness (2 Tim. 3:16); the preacher of the Word teaches

(2 Tim. 4:2). The Scripture corrects (2 Tim. 3:16); the preacher of the Word convinces and exhorts (2 Tim. 4:2). The Scripture reproves (2 Tim. 3:16); the preacher of the Word rebukes (2 Tim. 4:2). In other words, the preacher of the Word teaches, convinces, and rebukes.

From these and other passages, it is clear that God works through His Word. Jesus says, "Sanctify them by Your truth. Your word is truth" (Jn. 17:17). The Word of God is the truth of God that saves and sanctifies people. Moreover, God works through the *preaching* of His Word. He changes people through the *proclamation* of His message. When Jesus sent the disciples to preach, He told them God would speak through them (Mt. 10:7, 20).

Summary: God solemnly charges those who speak on His behalf to "preach the Word," that is, proclaiming *His* message, because, through the preaching of His Word, He saves and sanctifies people.

"Through the preaching of the Scriptures, God encounters men and women to bring them to salvation (II Tim. 3:15) and to richness and ripeness of Christian character (II Tim. 3:16-17). Something awesome happens when God confronts an individual through preaching and seizes him by the soul. The type of preaching that best carries the force of divine authority is expository preaching" (Robinson, pp. 18-19).

Chapter 2

Messages That Preach The Word

Most preachers don't preach *expository* messages. Most evangelicals cannot even agree on what it is. Strangely, everybody likes it, but only a few do it, and most do not even know how to define it! What is expository preaching?

A Popular Opinion

There is a great deal of confusion concerning the nature of expository preaching.

Verse-by-Verse Perhaps the most common conception of expository preaching is that it is preaching verse-by-verse. Expository preaching can be verse-by-verse, but moving from one verse to the next through a passage does not mean that the message is expository. The verse-by-verse view of exposition also leaves some questions unanswered. How many verses are in an expository message? Is it possible to preach an expository sermon on one verse?

Word-by-Word Some say that expository preaching is preaching through a passage word-by-word. This usually means explaining the meaning of Hebrew or Greek words, expounding on the parsing of Hebrew or Greek verbs, and elucidating on Hebrew or Greek syntax. Exposition may include references to the original text, but defining words, parsing verbs, and explaining syntax alone is not exposition.

Homiletical Textbooks

According to the dictionary, homiletics is the art of preparing and preaching sermons. Numerous textbooks have been written on homiletics. These textbooks should be the place to go for an accurate definition of expository preaching. What do they say? Textbooks on homiletics are unclear, or at least they do not agree among themselves as to what expository preaching is!

In his classic textbook on preaching, Broadus writes, "An expository discourse may be defined as one which is occupied mainly, or at any rate very largely, with the exposition of Scripture. It by no means excludes argument and exhortation as to the doctrines or lessons that this exposition develops. It may be devoted to a long passage, or to a very short one, even a part of a sentence. It may be one of a series or may stand by itself. We at once perceive that *there is no broad line of division between expository preaching and the common methods*, but that one may pass by almost insensible gradations from textual to expository sermons" (Broadus, p. 144, italics added).

Koller, the author of a book on expository preaching without notes, wrote, "Expository preaching is only one of several types of preaching which have been mightily used and mightily blessed of God. A study of the great sermons in sacred literature reveals *so much overlapping between these types as to make strict classification impossible*. Nor is it essential for any given sermon to be purely topical or purely textual or purely expository" (Koller, p. 28, italics added). Koller also says, "A 'Textual Sermon' is essentially the same as an 'Expository Sermon,' but employing a shorter Scripture passage, usually only a verse or a sentence or two. As generally conceived, it involves more intensive scrutiny of a less extensive passage. But many passages which should be treated as a unit are of such length as to make it *practically impossible to classify* the message as between textual and expository" (Koller, p. 22, italics added).

Davis, another professor on preaching, says, "The terms, topical, textual, and expository, are *used loosely and not at all uniformly* in homiletical literature, and *are of limited usefulness*" (Davis, p. 32, italics added).

A Suggestion

The key to exposition is *context*. Preaching the Word is proclaiming a message derived from the contextual study of Scripture. Therefore, such distinctions as word-by-word, verse-by-verse, and two or more verses are superficial. The issue is, "Was the message derived from the overall contextual message of the immediate passage and the larger context of that Scripture?" In other words, there are types of expositions.

Passage Exposition The exposition of a passage is the contextual explanation of several verses.

How to Hear God Speak
James 1:21-25

 I Put away sin
 II. Receive the Word
 III. Obey the Word
   Summary: The way to hear God speak is
   to put away sin and obey the Word of God.

Textual Exposition The exposition of a text, that is, a single verse, is the contextual explanation of that one verse. The danger of speaking on one verse is ripping the words of the verse from their context, thus making them mean something different from their original meaning. When, however, the contextual meaning of the verse is maintained, then "a textual message" is an expository message.

How to Be Happy

James 1:25

I. Carefully study the Word
II. Constantly meditate in the Word
III. Continually obey the Word

    Summary: The one who does
    what the Word says will be happy.

Topical Exposition The exposition of a biblical topic is the contextual explanation of that topic. Biographical exposition is also a type of topical exposition, as is evangelistic exposition.

The key to getting an Answer to Prayer

I. Believe (Mk. 11:24)
II. Abide in Christ and the Word (Jn.15:7)
II. Pray according to God's Word (1 Jn 5:14-15)

    Summary: The key to getting an answer to prayer is
    the Word of God. If the Word is abiding in you,
    then you will ask according to His will
    and thus be able to believe as you pray.

The issue in expository preaching is, "Is the message of the speaker the message of the passage (or passages) on which it is based?" The critical issue is *context*. It is possible to preach the Word from a single verse if the speaker's message is that verse's message in the passage's context. It is also possible to speak on one verse and not give the divine message of that verse.

For example, when the statement, "Where *there is* no vision, the people perish" (Prov. 29:18 KJV) is said to mean that if Christians do not have a vision for evangelism, people will go to hell, the speaker is putting words in God's mouth! That is not what Proverbs 29:18 means. God communicated to the prophets in the Old Testament through visions and dreams. Proverbs 29:11 says that people perish where there is no word from God. The entire verse says, "Where *there is* no vision, the people perish: but he that keepeth the law, happy *is* he" (Prov. 29:18 KJV). The New King James Version says, "Where *there is* no revelation, the people cast off restraint; but happy *is* he who keeps the law."

Perry and Whitesell say, "Definitions of expository preaching vary, but most of them indicate that its chief emphasis is an explanation of Bible passages and application of the truth. Expository preaching seeks to find the basic, *contextual-grammatical-historical* meaning of a passage of Scripture and then applies this meaning, by accepted rhetorical processes, to the hearts and lives of the hearers. Expository preaching finds more than a theme in a passage, more than a few suggestions, more than a few platitudes.—It finds the abiding message, the timeless truths, the universal values of the passage and brings them over in direct, powerful, impinging practical applications to modern life situations" (Whitesell and Perry, pp. 34-35, italics added).

Robinson says, "Expository preaching is the communication

of a biblical concept, derived from and transmitted through a historical, grammatical, and literary study of a passage in its *context*, which the Holy Spirit first applies to the personality and experience of the preacher, then through him to his hearers" (Robinson, p. 20, italics added).

Summary: Expository preaching is the communication of a biblical concept derived from the contextual study of a passage (or passages) of Scripture.

Most definitions are superficial. A person could deal with one verse and totally rip it from its context. Or a speaker could meticulously explain every detail in one or more verses and never explain the concept or message of that verse or passage. The critical issue in preaching the Word is preaching what God intended to say.

Chapter 3

Messages That Are Properly Prepared

An old recipe for a rabbit dish begins with the admonition, "First, catch the rabbit." To preach the Word, speakers must first understand the message of the Word so they can put that message in the form of a speech (sermon, lesson). That requires the preparation of biblical information.

The following procedure is for preparing a series of expository messages through a book of the Bible. It is also the method for preparing a single passage exposition, a verse exposition, or even a topical exposition. The topical exposition requires applying this method to every book where the topic appears. Topical messages demand more study because each reference to that topic must be studied in context.

This chapter is an edited version of some of the material from my book *How to Study the Bible*.

Survey the Historical Background

The place to start is with the historical background of the book.

Read the Book Read the book several times to determine the immediate historical situation. As you read, determine who wrote this book and to whom. Particular attention should be given to the conditions and circumstances of the recipients. In many cases, this is the key to understanding the book. For example, to understand the backdrop of Galatians, see Galatians 3:2; 4:10; 5:2; 6:12. Also, as you read, ask what is the subject of this book and why it was written.

Read Sources Read a reference Bible, a Bible Dictionary, and the introduction section of commentaries to confirm your conclusions and gain further insight. From these reference works, determine when the book was written and from where and to where.

Write a Summary This one-page, typewritten summary should answer the questions: Who wrote it? Who received it (especially their conditions)? When was it written? Where (that is, from where and to where)? What was written about (that is, the subject of the book), and why was it written?

Divide the Book into Literary Units

All literature has natural literary units, but there are different types of units depending on the type of literature.

Historical books The historical books in the Bible consist of individual *narratives*, which are often chapters. Joshua is an example.

Epistles In the New Testament, epistles consist of *paragraphs*. Paul's epistles are an example, as are general epistles such as James's.

There are no paragraph divisions in the original manuscripts of the New Testament. All paragraphs are man-made. Modern translations have divided the text into what the translators perceive to be proper paragraphing. Consequently, paragraph divisions differ from one translation to another. Natural paragraph divisions, not forced ones, are the ones to use.

Dividing a biblical book into its natural literary units gives the student a bird's eye view of the book rather than "a worm's eye analysis" (Robinson, p. 56).

Outline Each Unit

Once an overview of the book is in mind, determine the structure of each unit. There are several ways to do that.

Find the Literary Structure Within each literary unit, there is often a literary structure. Sometimes, the author's structure revolves around something specific. Here are some possibilities.

1. Places (Neh. 2)
2. People (Ps. 1, or relationships as in Col. 3:18-4:1; Titus 2:1-10)
3. Time (Neh. 1)
4. Commands (Col. 3:5-17, 4:2-6)
5. Repetition of a phrase (1 Jn. 1:5-2:2)
6. Subjects (Ps. 19:1-14)
7. Activities (Ps. 23; Mt. 28:16-20)
8. Questions (Dan. 12:5-13)
9. Reasons (1 Thess. 2:1-8)
10. Explanations (1 Thess. 4:13-17)

Determine the Major and Minor Ideas A passage of Scripture consists of a series of ideas. Some of those ideas are "major" concepts, and others support those major concepts. So ask, "What are the major 'points' in this passage and what is written that supports those points?"

The major points of Psalm 19 are: 1) The world reveals God's glory (Ps. 19:1). 2) The Word reveals God's plan (Ps. 19:7). 3) I want to please God (Ps. 19:12). All other verses support those points.

Construct an Interpretive Outline Of the different types of outlines (see examples below), an interpretive outline is the best one for communication purposes. It follows the order and content of the passage in its headings and subheadings. At the same time, it interprets the meaning of the passage in terms of today's significance.

1. Textual outline. A textual outline *uses the words of the text*. An outline should interpret the text, not just repeat the words of the text. A textual outline of Matthew 28:19-20 would look like this:

I. All authority is given to Me.
II. Make disciples among all nations.
   A. Going
   B. Baptizing
   C. Teaching.
III. Lo, I am with you always.

2. A literary analytical outline. A literary analysis outline *analyzes the literature*. An outline should interpret the text, not just analyze the literature of the text. Such an outline of Matthew 28:19-20 would look like this:

I. A Declaration
II. A Command
III. A Promise

3. An interpretive outline. An interpretive outline interprets the content of the unit for today. For example, an interpretive outline of Matthew 28:19-20 would be as follows:

   I. The authority of the Commission is Jesus Christ.
   II. The task of the Commission is to make disciples.
      A. Step one: initiation.
      B. Step two: identification.
      C. Step three: indoctrination.
   III. The power of the Commission is the spiritual presence of Christ.

Each point in the outline should be a complete sentence. This is in keeping with the concept that a literary unit contains ideas, not fragments.

Explain the Details

The next step is to explain the details of the passage. When done thoroughly, this complex process examines each sentence, clause, phrase, and word. Not all of those items in a portion of Scripture are significant. The object is to be able to explain the details of the passage in light of the overall context.

Study the passage before you look at any commentaries. Then, read at least three commentaries.

Summarize Each Passage

The "message" of each literary unit of Scripture can be summarized in one sentence; that is, each unit has a thesis (a message). Several critical questions need to be asked and answered to construct the message.

What is the Subject? The subject is the answer to the question, "What is the author talking about?" There are usually several topics in a unit of Scripture. Some are subordinate to others. There is always one subject to which everything is related or by which all is united. For example, let's suppose the subject is "sin."

What is the Narrowed Subject? A common pitfall is to assume that a single word is the subject of a unit. A single word is rarely, if ever, by itself a subject. It is tempting to say, for example, that the subject of a particular paragraph is sin, but no one paragraph covers all the aspects of sin, including its definition, its history, its causes, its results, its cure, etc.

The subject of a literary unit needs to be narrowed to a concise phrase so that the subject may be stated as clearly and accurately as possible. The subject of a paragraph is not just sin; it is the result of sin or the solution to sin.

What is the Author saying about the Narrowed Subject? Once the subject has been narrowed to a concise phrase, it should be completed and made into a complete sentence, a thesis (a message). If the subject is not completed, it is nothing more than a fragment, an open-ended phrase. The narrowed subject may be the result of sin. The message could be, "The result of sin is death." Or the narrowed subject could be "the solution of sin." The message would be, "The solution to sin is the blood of Jesus Christ."

The subject of 1 Corinthians 15:1-11 seems to be the gospel. In the opening verse, Paul says, "I declare to you the gospel" (1 Cor. 15:1). Then follows a series of phrases describing the gospel, but beginning at verse 3 through the end of the paragraph, Paul reveals the content of the gospel so that the narrowed subject seems to be "the content of the gospel by which we are saved." The message of the paragraph is "The content of the gospel by which we are saved is that Christ died for our sins and rose from the dead."

Why did the Author say that here? The context of a unit is the section of the book in which it is found. To "get at" the context of the unit, ask, "Why did the author say that here?" Asking that question will reveal the unit's context and often change your original message about the unit. It could even change the subject of the unit itself.

As an illustration, again, consider 1 Corinthians 15:1-11. The subject of this passage seems to be the gospel. In verse 1, Paul says, "I declare unto you the gospel." Then, he adds a series of phrases describing the gospel. Beginning at verse 3 through the end of the paragraph, he gives the content of the gospel. Therefore, the narrowed subject seems to be "The content of the gospel." The message is, "The content of the gospel is Christ died for our sins and rose from the dead."

Paul introduced that message here because the overall subject of 1 Corinthians 15 is Christ's resurrection from the dead. Paul is not talking about the gospel in isolation; he is talking about the gospel as it relates more specifically to the resurrection. When that fact is considered, it will be seen that the message in 1 Corinthians. 15:1-11 should be something like, "One of the great proofs for the resurrection is the gospel, which is that Christ died for our sins and rose from the dead."

Summary: To determine the biblical message, survey the historical background of the biblical book, divide the book into its natural literary units, outline each unit, explain the details in light of the context, and summarize each passage in a single summary sentence; that is, determine the message of the passage (the message). For a more detailed description of how to study a passage, see G. Michael Cocoris, *How To Study The Bible*.

To prepare an effective biblical message, you must first have a biblical message and a summary statement (a message). Now that the study of the passage is complete, the message itself needs to be prepared, but first, you need to analyze the audience.

Chapter 4

Messages That Are Effective

The speaker had a clear message. He could state his message in one simple sentence. He delivered well what he had prepared, but something was not right. His message did not hit home with the audience. In this case, the speaker had one purpose in mind: something he wanted to do, but it did not fit that audience that day. An effective message *fits the audience*.

In the book of Acts, after Paul was arrested, he gave several speeches in his defense. He delivered one to a riotous crowd in the Temple court (Acts 22:3-21). In another situation, Paul defended himself before Agrippa (Acts 26:1-23). Bruce remarks that the speeches cover the same ground to some extent, but "the general tone and atmosphere of the two speeches are different, each being adapted to its very distinctive audience." He adds that Paul's speech before Agrippa was designed to appeal particularly to the mind of Agrippa (Bruce, *The Book of Acts*, p. 461).

To produce effective messages, the speaker must analyze the audience and shape the message accordingly.

Analyze the Audience

The Occasion Analyzing an audience begins with examining the occasion of the meeting where you will speak.

What is the purpose of the meeting? Is it a regularly scheduled meeting or a special occasion? Will the people come primarily to hear you speak, or is your speech incidental to the purpose of the meeting? (Monroe, p. 179). Is this a Sunday morning church service? Is it an adult class? The reason for the meeting determines the expectations of the audience.

What will precede and follow your speech? What will take place before you speak? How long is the program before you speak? Will a meal be served? If so, will it be a light meal or a heavy meal? What is on the program after you speak?

Knowing the answer to all of these questions is important because you may be able to use other events on the program to your advantage. On the other hand, those events may work against what you have to say. So, you must consider the effects of the program as a whole and allow for it (Monroe, p. 180).

What will the physical conditions be at the meeting? Will the meeting take place inside or outside? If the meeting is out of doors, is it likely to be hot, cold, or comfortable? Will a public address system be used? Will the speaker be seen and heard easily? Is there likely to be outside noise or interruptions?

The answers to these questions could block the ability of the audience to listen to your speech. They could impact the way you approach your speech.

The Audience In his classic college textbook on speech, *Principles and Types of Speech*, Alan Monroe gives a number of factors to consider in an analysis of an audience (see Monroe, pp. 180-191):

1. The size of the audience.
2. The age of those making up the audience. Will the audience consist of young people, older people, people of the same age

level, or people of widely divergent ages?
3. The gender of the members of the audience. Will the audience be made up of men, women, or will it be mixed?
4. The occupations of the members of the audience. What is the socio-economic level of the audience?
5. The educational level of the members of the audience.
6. Membership in social, professional, and religious groups. Is a sizable part of the audience affiliated with some special group? What is their religious denomination?
7. The audience's knowledge of the subject. Will they understand technical terms without explanation?
8. The primary interest and desires of the audience. What do the people in your audience want most, and what are their chief interests?
9. The audience's attitudes and beliefs. What is the point of view of the audience? Audiences are usually made up of homogeneous groups. What ideas does this audience hold in common?

Knowing the audience's attitudes and beliefs can be helpful in several ways. For one thing, it will enable you to avoid arousing needless hostility. It may also enable you to show how your idea fits with an already accepted or how your proposal applies to some of their existing concepts.

10. The attitude of the audience toward the speaker. What will be the attitude of those in the audience towards you personally and toward your qualifications to address them on your subject? What is their degree of friendliness toward you and the degree of respect for you and your knowledge of the subject?
11. The attitude of the audience toward the subject. The people listening to your speech will either be interested in your subject or

apathetic. If they are apathetic, you will need to show them some connection to the subject that they have not realized, or you will need to arouse their curiosity about some novel aspect of the subject.

12. The attitude of the audience toward your purpose. Since audiences are never uniform, the answer to this question will consist of several different attitudes. At least determine the predominant attitude and adapt your speech accordingly.

The Thomas Nelson Publishing Company invited me to speak at two meetings on the East Coast, one in Pennsylvania and the other in Maryland. I was to speak on "The Case for the New King James Version."

The audience in the Philadelphia meeting consisted of a group of pastors, the majority of whom used the *King James Version* of the Bible. My assignment was to persuade them to consider the *New King James Version*. The audience in the small town in Maryland was made up primarily of Methodist ministers who use the *Revised Standard Version*.

There were vast differences between these two audiences. The people in one lived in a large metropolitan area, while those in the second resided in small-town America. The pastors in the first group were all African-American. Virtually all of the ministers in the second were Caucasian. The purpose of the meeting in Philadelphia was a regularly scheduled pastor's meeting. The purpose of the other meeting was the anniversary of the bookstore. These differences called for minor adjustments in the presentation.

The major difference between the two audiences, the version of the Bible they used, necessitated changing some of the material. One group needed information about why they should change from the *King James Version* to the *New King James Version*. Such information would have been of no value to the second group. They needed to know why they should switch from the *Revised Standard Version* to the *New King James Version*.

At the same time, the basic message remained the same. There is a case for the *New King James Version*, which needed to be presented to both audiences. Nevertheless, the differences in the audiences necessitated how the material was presented.

Decide the Purpose of the Message

The purpose of a speech is what the speaker wants to accomplish with a particular message on a particular occasion with a particular audience. Simply put, "The purpose of the message is what the speaker expects to happen in the hearers of the message" (Robinson, p. 108).

The prophets in the Old Testament and the authors of the New Testament spoke and wrote to a particular audience with a specific purpose. The book of Proverbs states its purpose at the beginning of the book (Prov. 1:1-4; also Jude 3). The gospel of John gives the purpose at the end of the book (Jn. 20:30-31). A purpose for writing can also appear in the middle of a book (1 Tim. 3:15).

As the prophets and preachers in the Scripture had a purpose for their message, so should the messenger of God today. Moreover, the purpose of biblical messages today should be in line with biblical purposes. The overall purpose of Scripture is to bring people to salvation (2 Tim. 3:15) and spiritual maturity (2 Tim. 3:16-17). More specifically, the purpose is to convict, instruct, enlighten, encourage, exhort, comfort, correct, and reproof. The expositor of the Scripture should first determine the purpose of a particular passage of Scripture. Then, decide what God desires to accomplish today through a message on that passage.

The purpose of a sermon is not unlike a professor's course objectives or a teacher's lesson plan. Modern educators are interested in measuring observable behavior change. Some speak of cognitive change involving knowledge and insight as well as affective change, including changes in attitudes and actions. The Scripture aims at those kinds of changes (Phil. 2:5; 2 Pet. 1:5-7).

The messenger of God's Word is not just dispensing information. The purpose of speaking for God is to impact those who hear. Plato speaks of a scholar who said, "When I listened to Pericles or any other orator of the day, I say to myself, 'He is a good speaker,' and that is all; but when I listened to Socrates, my soul is stirred, my eyes fill with tears, and I blush to the realities on which I spend my days" (Plato in *Symposium*).

With that in mind, speakers should write out the purpose of their speech. The message, which can be stated in a single sentence, does not change from audience to audience. However, The message's purpose may (and in some cases must) change from one audience to another. To a great extent, the purpose is determined by deciding what an audience needs concerning the message to be delivered to them.

Since the objective is to affect the listeners' lives, the purpose statement should be in terms of the listener. For example, if the purpose is knowledge, the purpose statement would say, "The listener should understand." The more specific the purpose statement, the better it is. For instance, if the purpose is to motivate believers to engage in evangelism, the purpose statement would be, "The listeners should understand their responsibility to spread the gospel and resolve to speak to at least one person about the Lord in the next week." Robinson observes, "Framing purposes that describe measurable results force the preacher to reflect on how attitudes and behavior should be altered. That, in turn, will enable him to be more concrete in his application of truth to life" (Robinson, p. 112).

Henry Ward Beecher said, "A sermon is not like a Chinese firecracker to be fired off for the noise it makes. It is a hunter's gun and at every discharge, he should look to see his game fall" (Beecher, quoted by Robinson, p. 108). As someone said, "The fact that a man shoots above the target only proves that he is a bad shot."

Determine the Direction of the Message

After carefully constructing the biblical message into a summary sentence and deciding on the purpose of the message, the next step is to determine the direction of the message. The need of the audience determines the direction of the message. Determining the direction can only be done in light of delivering a particular message to a particular audience. The critical issue is the audience. The question is, "What does this audience need?" The direction of the message is the "message need" of the audience. What are the possible directions a message can take? (see Robinson, pp. 79-96).

Explanation: This answers the question, "What does the biblical summary statement mean?" Some audiences only need an explanation of the passage. In many passages, some issues need explanation. The weaker brother in 1 Corinthians 8 is an example. So is the baptism of the Holy Spirit in 1 Corinthians 12:13.

Application: This answers the question, "What difference does it make?" An audience may already know the basic content of the biblical summary statement. An explanation might be so familiar it could bore them. They may need to be shown new or different ways to apply the message. While some explanation may need to be done, the bulk of the message will deal with how to implement the message.

In Ephesians 5, Paul tells husbands to love their wives (Eph. 5:25). Most male Christian audiences know that. What they need is instruction on how to apply that truth to their marriage. Paul himself gives two illustrations, which are applications of the general principle. The two illustrations are of Christ loving the church and a man loving his body.

Paul writes that husbands are to love their wives "just as Christ also loved the church and gave Himself for her" (Eph. 5:25). In other words, men are to sacrifice themselves for their wives. Later in the passage, Paul says, "So husbands ought to love their own wives as their own bodies; he who loves his wife loves himself. For no one ever hated his own flesh, but nourishes and cherishes it, just as the Lord *does* the church" (Eph. 5:28-29). Men should be as sensitive to their wives as they are to their own bodies.

Proof This answers the question, "Is it true?" An audience might not be convinced that the message is correct. They not only need it to be explained to them, they need to be persuaded that it is true. The proof can be Scripture, human authority (Titus 1:12), or common sense (1 Cor. 9:6-12).

The audience determines which type of proof is used. In Acts 2, Peter spoke to Jews, who accepted the Scripture as God's Word. Therefore, he quoted from the Old Testament. In Acts 17, when Paul spoke to the Greek intellectuals on Mars Hill, who did not accept the inspiration of the Old Testament, he did not quote it. Instead, he referred to their idols and philosophers.

Robinson concludes his discussion of the three developmental questions by saying, "While a preacher may deal with all three questions in his sermon, usually one of the three predominates and determines the form his message will take" (Robinson, p. 97).

Shape the Summary Statement to Fit the Audience

Having analyzed the audience, decided on the purpose and determined the "message need" of the audience, it is now time to shape the biblical statement into a sermon message. The message of a sermon is the summary of the sermon in a single sentence.

Start with the biblical message, that is, the summary statement of the biblical passage. It may be sufficient without many or any changes. It may be nothing more than putting the biblical message in the present tense and making it a universal statement.

Often, the biblical message needs to be simplified and made more memorable. For example, the subject of 1 Thessalonians 1:2-6 is thanksgiving for the believers at Thessalonica. Paul thanked God for them, giving two reasons: because of their effort and because of their election. The spiritual qualities in their lives inspired their effort. Being an example to other believers manifested their election. The biblical message statement is: "Paul thanked God for the effort and the election of the Thessalonians." A sermonic statement is: "Believers should thank God for what others have done for the Lord and for what the Lord has done for them."

Here is how Robinson handles that passage. His biblical summary statement is, "Paul thanked God for the Thessalonian Christians because of a result springing from their faith, hope, and love and because of the evidence of their election by God." His sermonic idea is, "We thank God for other Christians because of what they do for God and what God did for them" (Robinson, p. 98).

On the other hand, the biblical message may need to be shaped to fit the audience. That does not mean the biblical message changes; it means the message must be shaped to fit the audience.

The biblical message of John 3:1-16 is, "Jesus told Nicodemus, a Pharisee, he must be born again by faith." That biblical message statement could be shaped to fit a religious audience by changing it to read: "Even religious people need to be born again, by faith in Jesus Christ." After all, Nicodemus was a religious person; he was a Pharisee. It could also be shaped to fit a moral but not necessarily religious audience by changing it to say, "Even good people need to be born again by faith in Jesus Christ." As a Pharisee, Nicodemus was a moral person as well as a religious person. In neither of these cases does the biblical message change, but the message statement of the sermon states the biblical message to fit the audience.

Summary: To fit the biblical message to a particular audience, the speaker should analyze the audience, decide on a purpose, determine the "message need," and, with those issues in mind, shape the biblical message into a sermon message statement. Effective messages begin with a sermonic summary statement.

The purpose of Paul's message to husbands in Ephesians 5 is to motivate Christian husbands to love their wives. Based on the passage's purpose, the message might be for the listener to gain insight into how to love his wife and resolve to be sensitive to her needs in some specific way in the next 24 hours. If, however, the messenger knows there will be unsaved people in the audience, it would be perfectly appropriate to shape the message of Ephesians

5 to include salvation. After all, Paul went into detail about salvation (Eph. 2) before he discussed the marriage (Eph. 5). Thus, the purpose of the message would be for the listener to trust Christ and gain insight on how to love his wife resolving to be sensitive to her in some specific way, in the next 24 hours. The makeup of the audience did not change the biblical message, but it did shape it.

My message on James 1 was about how to handle trials. The first point was that you needed to rejoice. When I arrived at the service, I realized there were people in the audience who were facing a particularly heavy and grievous trial, the imminent death of a husband and father of young children. To begin with rejoicing would have turned them off for the rest of the message. So, I inverted the points of the message. Explaining how to handle the trial and then ending with rejoicing made the message more palatable, even to those facing severe trials.

Chapter 5

Messages That Are Clear

Have you ever heard a person deliver a speech and think to yourself, "What in the world is his point?" Or, "What is she trying to say?" Unfortunately, many preachers prepare and deliver foggy messages. Consequently, many people leave the church on Sunday morning in a cloud of confusion, unaffected by the message. As the Scripture says, "If the trumpet makes an uncertain sound, who will prepare for battle?" (1 Cor. 14:6-9).

What makes a message plain and powerful? The three characteristics of a clear, effective message are unity, order, and progress.

Unity

Unity Clarity begins with unity. Perhaps the most basic thing that can be said about a clear speech is that it has unity. A speaker who rambles or roams from one subject to another will be unclear and ineffectual. Rue says, "A work of art may express a variety of ideas, but it cannot remain a work of art unless this variety is held together by the unity of a single idea. The sermon, too, may and should present a variety of thoughts, yet it dare not be a barrage of heterogeneous and arbitrarily assembled elements but must form an organic unity" (Rue, p. 390).

Davis says, "When a sermon is the embodiment of one

vigorous idea, when the whole of it becomes simply the elaborating and extension of that idea, then it produces in the listener that concentration of effect, which is called unity.... Unity is not a sort of academic virtue prescribed by pedants for writers and speakers. Unity is a functional character of effective communication.... The desire for unity is a law of the listener's mind. It is his own sense of form at work, trying to bring order out of the chaos of impressions. If we do not combine our fragments into the wholeness we see, the listener's mind will force him to make his own combination of our fragments into a total impression that may be very different from our own. This is the imperative reason for unity."

Actually, this is common sense. We all recognize disunity when we hear it in a speech. A not-too-bright preacher decided to preach on Adam in the Garden of Eden. After pondering the passage, he came up with two points for a sermon. His first point was a question, "Adam, where art thou?" His second point was, "Adam, what are you doing there?" Thinking that no self-respecting preacher would only have two points in a sermon, he looked for a third. He could not find a third question in the passage, nor could he dream one up that fit the garden scene. So, he decided his third point should be "A word about baptism." Everyone recognizes that this is an inappropriate outline for a sermon because it lacks unity; there is incongruity in that sermon outline. Baptism was only thrown in as the third point. It had nothing intrinsically to do with the subject of the rest of the sermon. That may be an extreme case, but many preachers do something similar every Sunday.

The Message How does a speaker produce this essential element of unity? The universal answer given by speech teachers and homiletics professors is that properly using the concept of a "central idea" will achieve unity.

Messages That Are Clear

The sermons in Acts are illustrations of sermons with a single idea. Concerning the sermons in the book of Acts, Robinson says, "The sermons of the apostles were without exception, the proclamation of a single idea directed toward a particular audience" (Robinson, p. 36). Sunukjian concurs, saying, "Each of Paul's messages is centered around one single idea or thought. Each address crystallizes into a single sentence, which expresses the sum and substance of the whole discourse. Everything in the sermon either leads up to, develops, or follows a single unifying theme" (Sunukjian, cited by Robinson, p. 36).

For centuries, teachers of public speaking have argued that effective communication demands a single idea. Virtually all textbooks on public speaking teach this principle. The terminology varies. Some call it "the thesis statement" or "the theme." Others label it "the central idea," "the main thought," or "the proposition." Regardless of what it is called, the concept is the same: an effective speech consisting of one central idea (Robinson, pp. 33-34).

Since sermons are speeches, they should have a "central idea." The homiletics textbooks teach that a sermon should have one major idea.

Calling the "central idea" a proposition, Broadus says that it "is a statement of the subject as the preacher proposes to develop it. It is subject (idea) and predicate. The subject answers the question, 'What is the sermon about?' Fevelon put it this way, 'The discourse is the proposition unfolded, and the proposition is the discourse condensed. Its form should be one complete declarative sentence that is simple, clear, and cogent. It should contain no unnecessary or ambiguous words'" (Broadus, p. 54-55).

In his book *Design for Preaching*, H. Grady Davis agrees that the sermon must have unity, but he talks about "the idea" instead of "the proposition." He says, "A well-prepared sermon is the embodiment, the development, the full statement of a significant thought. Every thought is an idea, but a sermon idea is more than a bare thought. It is a thought plus its overtones and its groundswell is implication and urgency. It has more than the form of a thought; it has the energy, the life force of a thought. So it seems natural to speak of the 'idea' of a sermon.... In this sense, the idea of a sermon is the same thing as it is often inaccurately called a subject, topic, or theme. These words do not all mean the same thing and none of them any longer convey an exact sense. It seems more natural to call it the idea or the thought" (Davis, p. 20).

Robinson uses the expression "big idea." He says, "A sermon should be a bullet, not buckshot. Ideally, each sermon is the explanation, interpretation, and application of the single dominant idea supported by other ideas, all drawn from one passage or several passages of Scripture" (Robinson, p. 33).

Simply put, a sermon should have a "summary statement," which is another way to say a thesis. Every biblical passage has a summary statement (thesis). That biblical summary statement should be shaped into a sermonic summary statement (thesis).

Order

After unity, order is the next most essential element in an effective speech. Broadus points out that there must be order in the unity. He says, "All that is said might be upon the same subject, while the several thoughts by no means follow one another according to their natural relations" (Broadus, p. 97).

Broadus goes on to say, "Good order requires first of all that the various ideas comprising the unit of consideration be carefully distinguished from one another; secondly, that they follow one another in true sequence, so making for continuity and thirdly, that the order of thought shall move toward a climax" (Broadus, p.98).

Robinson says, "Sermons seldom fail because they have too many ideas; more often, they fail because they deal with unrelated ideas" (Robinson, p. 33).

Progress

The third fundamental factor in a powerful, persuasive speech is progress. Unity is like having a handful of pearls without having any jellybeans among them. Order is having all the pearls strung on a necklace. Progress is arranging the pearls from the smallest to the largest. Such an arrangement might not be appropriate for a pearl necklace, but progress is indispensable in a speech to keep people's attention and interest.

Without progress, the audience gets the impression that the speaker is treading water instead of swimming somewhere. As a result, their minds will begin to wander. They will lose concentration. Consequently, the message will be unclear to them. Thus, progress is necessary for a clear message.

Summary: Effective messages are clear; that is, they have unity, order, and progress.

Napoleon issued three commands to his messengers: "Be clear! Be clear! Be clear!" A clear message has unity; it can be stated in a single sentence. Then, that summary statement is developed in an orderly and progressive manner.

Messages are unclear to an audience because they are first

unclear to the speaker. They are usually unclear to the speaker because he or she is thinking in terms of fragments and not complete thoughts.

If you are to speak clearly, you must think through exactly what you are going to say. Your "message" must be stated in a single, concise, clear sentence. Frankly, this is hard work. It takes time and effort, but it is well worth the investment. It can also be discouraging. Trying to "fit" every idea into one main idea is often frustrating.

J. H. Jowett says, "No sermon is ready for preaching ... until we can express its theme in a short, pregnant sentence as clear as crystal. I find getting that sentence the hardest, most exacting and most fruitful labor in my study. To compel oneself to fashion that sentence, to dismiss every word that is vague, ragged, ambiguous, to think oneself through to a form of words that defines the theme with scrupulous exactness—that is surely one of the most vital and essential factors in the making of a sermon: and I do not think any sermon ought to be preached or even written until that sentence has emerged clear and lucid as a cloudless moon" (Jowett. p.133).

Robinson concludes, "If a preacher will not—or cannot—think himself clear so that he says what he means, he has no business in the pulpit. He is like a singer who can't sing, an actor who can't act, an accountant who can't add" (Robinson, p. 39).

Chapter 6

Messages That People Can Follow

As two men listened attentively to a passionate pastor, one turned to the other and said, "He lost me! What is he talking about now?" Many others in the congregation thought something similar; they just didn't say anything.

Unfortunately, many messengers deliver messy messages that audiences cannot follow. As a result, the audience gets lost. Worse yet, the audience fails to get the message, or if it is clearly stated somewhere towards the end, it fails to have the same impact it could have had if the audience had stayed with the speaker throughout the presentation.

To prevent the audience from getting lost and to help the audience follow the speaker, he must clearly develop his thesis. An effective message has unity, that is, it is a discourse on a single subject, but a single subject has various parts. The development is the structure, that is, the arrangement of those parts. The common name is outline. Effective communication makes the message's development (structure) clear to the audience.

For the effective development of a message, follow these three steps.

The Development of the Overall Message

With the message clearly in focus and a definite audience in mind, the next step is to decide on the type of development to deliver the message to that particular audience. In other words, determine the outline of the overall message. This outline creates the main point of the outline. In the following list of types of developments, the first three are the most common.

Deductive Development In deductive development, the *idea* is stated somewhere at the beginning of the message, usually at the end of the introduction. Then, the *development*, that is, the outline, explains the idea, proves the idea, illustrates the idea, etc.

In Acts 13, Paul develops his message deductively, beginning with the statement, "From this man's seed, according to *the* promise, God raised up for Israel a Savior, Jesus" (Acts 13:23). After Paul made his main point, all that follows supports it.

When the audience needs explanation and the thrust of the sermon is explaining the message of a passage of Scripture, an excellent approach is the old rule: "Tell them what you are going to tell them. Tell them. Then tell them what you told them." In the introduction, usually toward the end of it, the summary statement is stated. In the body of the message, the speaker explains the message, point by point. In the conclusion, the summary statement is repeated.

Inductive Development Inductive development is the opposite of deductive development. Inductive development gives the development, that is, the outline first and then states the idea as the logical conclusion.

When facing an antagonistic audience, Peter developed his message inductively. He did not state his conclusion until the end of his message, when he finally said, "Therefore let all the house of Israel know assuredly that God has made this Jesus, whom you crucified, both Lord and Christ" (Acts 2:36).

Developmental Development A developmental approach is what its name implies. Instead of stating the thesis statement of the message at the beginning or the end, it is "developed" bit by bit throughout the speech. In most expository messages, the outline of the message follows the outline of the passage in its main points and sub-points. Expository messages, however, do not have to follow the outline of the passage.

In his book *Biblical Preaching*, Robinson discusses other ways to develop the summary statement of the message.

Explaining an Idea Robinson states, "A clear explanation of a biblical passage may be the most important contribution an expositor can make in his sermon." He also says, "A truth correctly comprehended carries its own application" (Robinson, p. 116). This type of development pattern is the same as the deductive development mentioned above.

Prove a Proposition When the audience needs the passage's message to be proven to them, the summary statement is stated in the introduction, and the points in the body of this message are proofs or reasons for the summary statement. Again, this is a deductive type of development.

Apply a Principle If the audience needs application, the summary statement should be stated in the introduction, and the various points in the body of the message are applications of it. Once again, this is a deductive type of development.

Complete a Subject According to Robinson, this is the most common form of development. The subject, but not the entire idea, is stated in the introduction. The major points of the message complete the subject. Each major point is not necessarily related to the previous point, only to the subject that it completes. This is a form of the developmental development mentioned above.

Explore a Problem In this development of the summary statement, a question or problem is posed in the introduction. The first major point explores adequate solutions. The second point is the summary statement of the message. It is the answer to the question or the solution to the problem presented in the introduction. The remainder of the message explains, defends, or applies the solution.

Tell a Story In this approach, the whole message is in story form. When done with insight and imagination, making the whole sermon a story is a powerful way to deliver a message. Like other sermons, this type consists of a major idea supported by other ideas. The difference, of course, is that those points are made with the story.

Stories are not just for children. Adults get absorbed in novels and are addicted to TV shows, not to mention movies. The greatest speaker who ever lived, Jesus Christ, was a storyteller. As a speaker, Jesus Christ is known for His parables. So, do not shortchange storytelling.

Whatever type of development is used, each point should be a complete sentence. The point that consists of only a word, several words, or a phrase is incomplete and, therefore, vague.

The all-too-common practice among preachers of producing a one-word alliterative outline has caused more than one to think in fragments. The outline, at least the one from which the preacher works out in his study, should consist of complete sentences. It will clarify in his mind exactly what he wants to say so that he can clearly communicate to his audience. Then, perhaps, those sentences can be abbreviated to a one-word or short phrase outline to be taken into the pulpit, but each word or phrase in that outline should represent a complete sentence.

The Development of the Major Points

After the development of the overall message, develop each major point. The development of one point may differ dramatically from the point just before it or the one immediately following it. Again, where the audience is and or what the audience needs in relation to a particular point dictates how that point is developed. The same types of developments that apply to the overall message are used to develop each point. Beyond those, other major development points include the following:

Components Pattern Perhaps the most natural way to develop a major point in a message is to take the various sub-points in the major point and develop them one by one. This approach resembles the developmental pattern mentioned above.

Implications Pattern The development of a point may have a series of implications.

The Contrast Pattern The contrast pattern gives the contrast (or contrasts) to the point being made.

The Refutation Pattern The refutation pattern refutes possible objections to the point.

The Application Pattern The sub-points under a main point may be an application (or applications) of the main point.

Regardless of the sub-point pattern, the application can and should appear throughout the message. "An expository preacher confronts people about themselves from the Bible instead of lecturing to them from the Bible about history or archaeology. A congregation convenes as a jury not to convict Judas, Peter, or Solomon, but to judge themselves" (Robinson, p. 27).

As with the main point, the sub-points should be complete sentences.

Transitions

The key to a clear outline is the transition between the points. Transitions are needed between the introduction and the body of the message, between the points within the body, and between the body and the conclusion.

The difference between amateurs and seasoned speakers is transitions. Inexperienced speakers move from one point to another without telling their audience what they are doing. Consequently, the audience gets lost. Effective speakers never forget that they must take their audience with them through their outline.

An effective transition notifies the audience that the speaker is moving from one point to another. That can be done in many different ways. One of the simplest ways is to announce at the end of the introduction that you have x number of points. Then, as you move through the message, at the beginning of each point, state the number of that point.

Without using numbers, an effective transition can be made by reviewing what has been said and announcing what will be said next. Of course, the transition can be made without reviewing the last point. Just make a simple announcement of the new point.

Do not be afraid of repetition (2 Pet. 3:1). "To nail a truth into the mind requires that we hit it several times" (Robinson, p. 149).

Summary: Effective messages are messages audiences can follow; they have a designed development with clear transitions.

The development of a message is like a skeleton in a body. A jellyfish has no skeleton. It just floats, being carried along by the current. Fish with skeletons move by design toward a place of their choosing.

As a rule, it is only possible for a speaker to make about six points in thirty minutes.

Chapter 7

Messages That Keep People's Attention

Having a message that is stated in a single sentence (message) and having a definite purpose as well as an appropriate development will produce clear messages, but clear messages are not necessarily effective. Clear messages can bore people to the point of putting them to sleep. Effective messages contain material that holds people's attention.

A message's development, or "outline," is like a skeleton. A skeleton may be clear, but uninteresting. In terms of a message, "flesh" must be added to the skeleton. In other words, after a point is stated, a speaker must use material that will effectively communicate that point to the audience. This material is sometimes called "support material." It supports the various points. It is the flesh of the message.

Explanation

One of the most basic things a speaker can do to support his point is to explain it. If an audience does not understand the message, that is, if they need more explanation, the message will not be effective.

Explanations include the definition of terms, a discussion of terms, comparisons, contrast, the significance of the subject, the implications of the topic at hand, the consequences of the issue, the relationship of this idea to another idea, etc. For example, in preaching on John 3, explaining the new birth would not only be appropriate, but it would be essential to proclaim the passage's message clearly. Our first at birth is physical. Our second birth is spiritual.

Keep it Simple The first rule for using explanation is to keep it simple and short. An old, oft-repeated story is about the wife of the speaker who passed her husband a note just before he got up to speak. It read, "K.I.S.S." He thought it was a loving send-off to the platform. He later learned that her note reminded him to "Keep it simple, stupid." K.I.S.S. also means "keep it short, stupid."

Know it Well The second rule is "know it well." You ought to be able to explain your points in private conversation. If you cannot explain your points in a private conversation without notes, you are not ready to explain them publicly. If you want the acid test of whether or not you can clearly explain an idea, try explaining it to older children or, if it is more abstract, to teenagers. As a rule, if teenagers do not get it, they will let you know.

Rarely Enough The third rule for the explanation is to remember that seldom is enough by itself. On the one hand, some explanation is usually needed. On the other hand, if it is all you have, you probably do not have enough.

Factual Information

The most effective messages consist of carefully chosen facts. Indeed, exhortation, which is extremely difficult to do, is effectively done when based on clearly seen facts. Speeches, therefore, should be tastefully seasoned with factual information.

Definition What is sometimes paraded as "a matter of fact" is, in reality, only a matter of opinion. According to the dictionary, facts are something having their existence supported by evidence. Facts are data verified apart from the speaker (Robinson, p. 141).

Examples Facts consist of observations, examples, statistics, etc.

Unless there is a compelling reason (a technical detail where one number would make a difference), if you use statistics containing more than four figures, round off the number. For example, instead of saying 1389, say about 1400.

Figures by themselves tend to be uninteresting to most people, so when using statistics, use a comparison. It is also helpful to relate figures to experience.

If the figures you are using are doubtful, meaning you either you cannot verify them or they sound doubtful to most people, give the source and, if possible, a date.

Needless to say, if you are going to use facts, make sure they are facts. If you have any doubt, research. Use the Internet, but make sure the source is reliable. Most public libraries have a department that gives you material on just about any subject. Do not hesitate to call a library to verify the facts you intend to use in a speech. Bernard Baruch says, "Every man has a right to his own opinion, but no man has a right to be wrong in his facts" (Robinson, p. 142).

Quotation

Use quotations for one of two reasons: authority and impressiveness.

Authority If you are not qualified to speak on a subject, quote an expert. Make sure the expert is qualified to speak on the subject. Also, make sure the expert is not prejudiced. If the authority is unknown to the audience, give his or her qualifications to speak to the issue.

Impressiveness If someone else has stated an idea more eloquently or effectively, you can use that person's words. Quotations should be brief.

First Timothy 3:4 says that an elder must be "one who rules his own house well, having *his* children in submission with all reverence." In other words, an elder must rear his children with reverence. The Greek word translated "reverence" means "reverend, venerable, grave, serious." It consists of a sense of gravity and dignity, which invites reverence (Trench, pp. 346-348). Hendrickson puts it like this: "Authority must be exercised, but this must be done 'with true dignity,' that is, it must be done in such a manner that the father's *firmness* and make it *advisable* for the child to obey, but his *wisdom* makes it *natural* for a child to obey and that his *love* makes it a *pleasure* of the child to obey."

Take another example. Clarence McCartney said, "The motto for every earnest minister ought to be that of the Great Minister, the Great Shepherd, Himself, Who said, 'For their sakes I sanctify Myself.' The better the man, the better the preacher. When he kneels by the bed of the dying or when he mounts the pulpit stairs, then every self-denial he has made, every Christian forbearance he has shown, every resistance to sin and temptation will come back to him to strengthen his arm and give conviction to his voice. Likewise, every evasion of duty, every indulgence of self, every compromise with evil, and every unworthy thought, word, or deed will be there at the head of the pulpit stairs to meet the minister on Sunday morning to take the light from his eye, the power from his blow, the ring from his voice, and the joy from his heart."

So, use quotations when the quoted person has more authority than you or says it better than you would. When using a quotation, put it on an index card and keep it short. Use quotations rarely.

Testimony

Someone's testimony is a common method speakers use to buttress the point they are trying to make. Some overdo it, but it can be effective.

Qualifications If you use someone else's testimony, make sure the person is qualified on the subject. Television commercials violate this principle frequently. For example, Bart Starr was a famous quarterback for the Green Bay Packers. Years ago, he was featured in a commercial that said, "Bart Starr takes chances on the field but never with his anti-freeze." Frankly, as great a football star as Bart Starr was, that did not qualify him as an expert on anti-freeze. A football player's opinion on anti-freeze is no better than a mechanic's opinion on who will win the next Super Bowl.

Questions Before using testimonies, ask, "Is the person's statement based on first-hand knowledge? Is the person prejudiced? Does the audience respect the person?"

A reporter once asked Billy Graham, "If you had your life to live over again, would you do some things differently?" Graham responded, "Yes." On being asked what he would do differently, Graham said, "I would spend more time studying the Bible." Coming from Billy Graham, that is a powerful testimony.

Narration

When correctly done, narration can be one of the most effective means of communicating a message because it appeals to the imagination. It is simply narrating a story instead of explaining a point. A story has been defined as a character at war. Conflict is at the heart of the essence of a story.

Story Telling The simplest way to tell a story is to follow—in order—the four parts of story development. Story development consists of characters, conflict, complications, and conclusion. In other words, first, introduce the characters. Then, talk about the conflict, add complications, and conclude by resolving the conflict.

Helpful Tips Take the viewpoint of one character. Develop the plot swiftly and accurately. Use imagination. Use dialogue. Put words into characters' mouths. If only one person is involved in the story, use soliloquy or self-talk (Lk. 16:2-7; 15:11-32).

While narration can be a powerful message communication tool, limitations exist. Narration is not a good way to teach new material. Furthermore, it demands active listeners to catch deep meanings.

> Give me a fact and I will learn
> Give me a truth and I will remember
> Tell me a story and I'll keep it in my heart forever.
> (source unknown)

Illustrations

An illustration is a story that explains a truth through comparison or contrast. Illustrations can be the most effective means of communicating a message. They are powerful. They render truth believable. They hold attention, establish rapport between the speaker and hearer, enlighten the mind, stir emotions, and aid memory. For the most effective use of illustrations, follow these principles.

Understandable First, make sure the illustration is understandable. The point of an illustration is to clarify the unknown with the known. Therefore, the most understandable illustrations deal with experiences that the speaker and the audience have had. The next most likely understandable illustration deals with the speaker's experience and about which the audience has knowledge. The least understandable illustrations contain material the speaker and the audience know about but have not experienced.

Believable For an illustration to be convincing, it must be believable. If an illustration strikes an audience as unbelievable, it will affect the speaker's credibility.

Pertinent Illustrations must be pertinent to the point. Do not use an illustration for the sake of having an illustration. It will detract from the point, if it is irrelevant to the point.

Interesting Illustrations must have interest value. Avoid familiar illustrations. Leave out unnecessary words.

In the preaching labs I conducted at Dallas Seminary, I often asked students, "Who was the greatest speaker who ever lived?" Being biased seminarians, they said, "Jesus Christ." I then inquired, "When you think of Jesus Christ as a speaker, what is the first thing that comes to mind?" The answer is obvious—parables. The greatest speaker who ever lived is known for telling stories. So, I said, "When you speak, make sure you are Christ-like. Tell a story. To speak without telling stories is ungodly!"

Jesus Christ chose His stories from nature, agriculture, current events, personal experience, the religious world, the political world, the business world, social customs, household customs, family relationships, and the human body. He used them to answer questions, introduce messages, explain concepts, state truth, hide truth, and conclude a message (G. Michael Cocoris, *Christ's Use of Illustrations*, unpublished Master's Thesis, Dallas Theological Seminary, 1966).

For most speakers, the biggest difficulty with using illustrations is finding them. To find illustrations, first look at your own experience or other people's experiences. Look in books, booklets, magazines, and newspapers on your subject. Google it. Spurgeon says, "All originality and no plagiarism makes for dull preaching." If all else fails, make up a story. Jesus told parables, which were nothing more than hypothetical stories.

Summary: Effective messages keep people's attention by using various kinds of material to support the points of the message.

There are many other ways to support a point. The following is a list of items we have discussed and other things you can do to communicate a point effectively. When preparing a message, keep this list handy.

1. Definitions: What does a word mean?
2. Explanations: What does this concept mean?
3. Factual Information: What fact supports this idea?
4. Quotation: What authority confirms this contention?
5. Testimony: Who has experienced this truth?
6. Narration: How can this be dramatized?
7. Illustration: What story communicates this truth?
8. Applications: What you should do.
9. Reasons: Why should you do this?
10. Gains: What you will gain if you do this.

11. Losses: What you will lose if you don't do this.
12. Excuses: Why people don't do this.
13. Opposites: What is the opposite of this?
14. Alternatives: What you could do besides this.
15. Humor: What about this is absurd?

The outline of a message is the skeleton of a message. A skeleton without flesh is dead. To keep people interested, there must be more to look at than bare bones. Adding support material puts flesh on the bones. Insights breathe life into the body.

Chapter 8

Messages That Move People's Feet

The plane speeds down the runway, slowly lifts off the ground, and becomes airborne. The flight itself is uneventful, which is how all aboard wanted it, but as everyone knows, a flight is not complete or successful until the plane lands safely. Indeed, unless the plane lands properly, little else matters.

A speech is like an airplane flight. The takeoff (the introduction) and the flight (the body of the speech) do not guarantee a successful landing (conclusion). While there may still be benefits to a message with a weak conclusion, needless to say, the message would be more effective with a powerful conclusion.

The Purposes of a Conclusion

"The purpose of the conclusion is to conclude—not merely to stop." It should produce a feeling of finality (Robinson, p. 167). Often, the conclusion is the emotional high point of the message.

Focus the Message One of the major purposes of a conclusion is to bring the message into focus. Hopefully, by the time a speaker arrives at his conclusion, the audience has gotten the message, but as experienced speakers know, no matter how attentive the audience seems to be, some in the audience are slower to get the message than others. So play it safe. In the conclusion, clearly expose your central idea. In other words, state your sentence summary of the message. As a rule, speakers should state their sentence summary somewhere in the message one or more times. If such a statement has not been given before the conclusion, it should be done in the conclusion.

The only exception to not clearly stating a summary sentence of the message is when dealing with a highly sophisticated audience who can be counted on to get the message even though it is not stated. Stories sometimes contain this technique. When done properly with the right audience, it can be very powerful.

Apply the Message Another purpose of almost all messages is to apply the message to the audience. The application relates the message to the individuals in the audience. For example, if the message is "a penny saved is a penny earned," it would conclude one way with adults and another way with young people. The speaker to adults might talk about saving money for next year's vacation, while the same speaker addressing young people might talk about saving money for weekly entertainment.

Write out the conclusion with the purpose in mind. Be specific. Don't forget to include specific suggestions for behavioral change.

Obtain a Decision: Some speeches just dispense data. The purpose of the conclusion is to obtain a decision. It is to move people to action. Lybrand observes, "At its heart, preaching is about persuasion," and "Preaching is actually about winning the listener to think, feel, and act in accordance with the biblical truth at hand" (Lybrand, p. 27). As an old, experienced preacher told a friend of mine, "I tell them what I want them to know, feel, and do."

According to the ancient Greeks, persuasion includes ethos, logos, and pathos. Ethos is the ethic, the credibility of the speaker. Logos is the logic and reasonableness of the evidence. The pathos is the speaker's passion; it is the emotional element. The preacher of the Word must have character, credibility, and believability. Robinson says, "Ultimately, God is more interested in developing messengers than messages" (Robinson, p. 25). The message should make sense. If it is to persuade, it must be reasonable to the listener. Persuasion also includes emotions. Emotion may occur at any point in the sermon. There can be laughter at a joke or tears at a story. Some speakers work on people's emotions. That can be manipulation. At the same time, the reality is that people are emotional creatures. Emotions have a place in preaching and persuasion.

After the service, as I was leaving, I came upon two ladies talking to each other. I paused to greet them when one of them said, "We are so glad you are our pastor." The other commented, "You make us laugh and cry." I do not design my messages with those things in mind, but I am aware that some sermon material lends itself to provoking laughter and tears, and when I find material that *fits the exposition of the passage*, I do not hesitate to use it. That's important. The goal is to communicate the truth of the text. I only use illustrative material that accomplishes that end. I've never put anything in a sermon that has emotion but does not fit. I have not always been able to produce sermons that have emotional appeal, which helps people relate to the speaker and drive home the point. The purpose is not to entertain but to impact people with truth as forcefully as possible; emotion is an effective way to do that.

How do you obtain a decision? There are many principles that speakers and salesmen have used to bring people to the point of a decision. One of the most basic is to assume the decision has been made. In sales, this approach is called "the assumptive close." A salesperson, assuming the customer is going to buy, says to the customer, "You need to make out the check to so and so for a specific amount of money." Similarly, speakers may assume that they have convinced the audience and conclude by telling them what to do.

On the other hand, perhaps the most basic way to obtain a decision is to ask for it. In sales, this is called "requesting the order." Likewise, speakers could conclude with, "Will you make a decision today to _____?"

Many audiences need more than information or a request. Thus, you may need to do one of several other things. You may need to summarize the benefits. An individual must be convinced that the value exceeds the price to decide in favor of what you are "selling." So, focus on all the individual will get if he or she makes the decision you suggest.

Another possibility is to answer excuses. In sales, this refers to as "overcoming objections." In fact, some have suggested that the essence of selling, that is, obtaining a decision, is overcoming objections. To do this most effectively, speakers must know the objections their message will raise.

Perhaps one of the most effective principles in obtaining a decision is to give the audience a choice. In other words, ask a question, but instead of designing the question so that the listener can give a yes or no response, craft the question in such a way that the listener would normally respond with a choice. For example, in sales, instead of asking, "Would you like to buy this?" you would say, "Would you like to buy this one or that one?" In a sermon, instead of saying, "Would you like to trust Christ?" ask, "Would you rather go to heaven or hell?" Moses, Joshua, and Jesus used this method.

Just before he died, Moses preached a series of sermons we call Deuteronomy. At the end, he said, "See, I have set before you today life and good, death and evil, in that I command you today to love the LORD your God, to walk in His ways, and to keep His commandments, His statutes, and His judgments, that you may live and multiply; and the LORD your God will bless you in the land which you go to possess. But if your heart turns away so that you do not hear, and are drawn away, and worship other gods and serve them, I announce to you today that you shall surely perish; you shall not prolong *your* days in the land which you cross over the Jordan to go in and possess. I call heaven and earth as witnesses today against you, *that* I have set before you life and death, blessing and cursing; therefore choose life, that both you and your descendants may live; that you may love the LORD your God, that you may obey His voice, and that you may cling to Him, for He *is* your life and the length of your days; and that you may dwell in the land which the LORD swore to your fathers, to Abraham, Isaac, and Jacob, to give them" (Deut. 30:15-20).

At the end of his life, Joshua delivered a farewell address at the end of which he said, "And if it seems evil to you to serve the LORD, choose for yourselves this day whom you will serve, whether the gods which your fathers served that *were* on the other side of the River or the gods of the Amorites, in whose land you dwell. But as for me and my house, we will serve the LORD" (Josh. 24:15).

At the conclusion of the Sermon on the Mount, Jesus said, "Enter by the narrow gate; for wide *is* the gate and broad *is* the way that leads to destruction, and there are many who go in by it. Because narrow *is* the gate and difficult *is* the way which leads to life, and there are few who find it" (Mt 7:13-14).

Convincing people that they need to do something and getting them to decide to do it *now* are two different things. Therefore, those most successful at persuasion know that they need to add the element of urgency. One way to do that is to say, "You need to do this now." The other way is to tell a person why such a decision needs to be made *now* instead of later.

Study the Scripture. Speak with passion. Preach for a decision.

Types of Conclusions

Formal Most messages use a formal conclusion. A formal conclusion reviews the whole message after the last point has been developed. Use this type of conclusion when the last point doesn't encompass the entire idea of the message. In this type of conclusion, no new material is used in the sense of new ideas.

Last Point Conclusion Another type of conclusion is the last point conclusion. This type of conclusion should be used when the last major point states the whole idea. In this type of conclusion, after the development of the last point, the speaker gives implications, applications, exhortations, etc. New material is often introduced.

Methods of Conclusions

Summary The recapitulation of the major points is appropriate, especially when the goal is to inform or inspire. While restatement of the major points may be a helpful technique to focus the message, it is usually weak by itself. It does not apply the message, nor does it attempt to obtain a decision.

Exhortation Many, probably too many, preachers, persuaders, and public speakers conclude with direct exhortation. Direct exhortation has a place, but exhorting people in general is very difficult. Direct exhortation, especially to a sophisticated audience, can be a "turn off" instead of a "turn on." So, while direct exhortation is one possible method of concluding a message, it should be done tactfully and tastefully. It can be overdone.

Suggestions In most instances, it would probably be more effective for speakers to give specific suggestions for carrying out the idea. Be specific. Start with little suggestions. Build toward a big suggestion.

An illustration Because everyone likes a story, a message that concludes with an illustration that applies the message can be very effective. The illustration or story can apply either the idea of the whole message or the last point.

Contrasting Truth For some messages, the most appropriate way to conclude is with the contrasting truth. A sermon on hell should conclude with a word about heaven. A message dealing with problems should conclude with possible solutions.

Visualization: Instead of illustrating the message from someone else's life, why not conclude with a visualization concerning a typical audience member? Begin the visualization by constructing a situation. Put an imaginary individual who is typical of individuals in the audience in the story. Then, show how your message would work for that individual in that situation. For this method to be effective, the visualization must be true to life and as specific as possible (see Monroe, pp. 327-329).

Quotation Conclude the message with a quotation. The quotation may consist of something someone has said, a poem, a hymn, a popular song, etc. The quotation should be short and to the point.

A Rhetorical Question A message could conclude with a rhetorical question, which asks a question that does not expect an audible answer. A question or a series of questions helps the listener participate in the message.

A rhetorical question can be used by itself as the whole conclusion, but in most cases, it is probably more effective if used in combination with one of the other methods, perhaps as the last statement uttered. A pastor concluded his message with the question, "Are you dead, deceived, or dangerous for God?"

Summary: Effective messages contain conclusions that focus, apply, and usually obtain a decision for the message using various methods.

An airplane flight may be pleasant and perfect, but it is not considered a successful flight if it does not have a safe landing. Delivering a speech may not be dramatic, but if a speech does not have an effective conclusion, it is usually ineffective.

Chapter 9

Messages That Grab People By Their Ears

When you meet someone for the first time, you immediately begin to form impressions of that person. The very first impressions are based on non-verbal observations like their appearance. Then, you form opinions about the person based on what he or she says. Those first impressions are critical. They can determine whether or not you wish to continue conversing with this person.

The introduction of a message is as important as a first impression. It can easily determine whether or not the audience will be motivated to listen to the remainder of what you have to say. Like meeting a person for the first time, the introduction of a speech consists of non-verbal as well as verbal elements. The non-verbal elements begin before the speaker opens his or her mouth. The verbal elements, of course, are the introduction itself. With that in mind, the question becomes, how do you prepare an effective introduction?

The Purposes of Introductions

In the broadest sense of the term, introducing a speaker to the audience has two purposes. The first is to relate the audience to the speaker, and the second is to relate the audience to the subject of the speech. Virtually all the first purpose is accomplished before the speakers open their mouths or at least before they begin the message. The second purpose is accomplished in what is generally thought of as the introduction of the message.

Methods of Relating an Audience to a Speaker

The following are suggestions for how to relate the audience to the speaker.

Be Properly Dressed If you are a man and the occasion calls for wearing a suit, unless there is not a compelling reason for doing otherwise, you should wear either a dark blue or gray suit. Research has confirmed that blue and gray project authority and credibility. The reason for this is tradition. In Western civilization, those in authority, such as politicians, attorneys, bankers, and executives, have traditionally worn dark blue and gray almost exclusively. Make sure that your clothes fit properly. Poorly fitted clothes, especially clothing that is too small, will attract attention and distract the message. A man giving a speech in a suit should wear a long-sleeved shirt. If he sits on the platform, he should wear over-the-calf socks. Books have been written on proper business dress for men and women. If you have not done so, you should read at least one. Start with *Dress for Success* by John T. Molloy.

Be Sensitive to the Congregation During the part of the program before the message, most speakers concentrate on their message. That is not necessarily all bad. However, you are in trouble if you are not prepared at that point! So, take at least a few minutes to think about your audience. Put yourself in their place. Try to understand them. Remember, everyone there has a problem. Everyone there has a need. Hopefully, if not everyone, then the majority need what you say. Think of them as people who need what you are about to tell them and adopt the attitude of expecting them to respond positively to your message.

Beware of negative attitudes, such as, "The attendance is not what I expected." Your attitude, whether positive or negative, will subtly seep through to the audience and affect your message. The people who came to hear you speak should not have to pay for the ones who didn't. At least think favorably about those who honored you with their presence.

Be Introduced Properly The rule of introducing a speaker to the audience is that the introduction should build the audience's confidence in the speaker. More specifically, an introduction should give the speaker's qualifications for speaking on the subject of the speech. Why should this audience listen to this speaker talk about this subject? The speaker's education, experience, or both can be used to demonstrate his or her qualifications.

The speaker's name should be clearly stated twice: once at the beginning of the introduction and again at the end. It is also helpful for the one introducing the speaker to add a personal touch by commenting favorably on something about the speaker's person and/or his or her relationship to the speaker.

Do not hesitate to tell the person who will introduce you what to say. Do not assume that just because this person has been chosen to introduce you, he or she has been given the least bit of instruction on how to do it. Additionally, give the introducer a typewritten list of your qualifications. Having been introduced hundreds of times literally from coast to coast, from border to border, and beyond, I can tell you from experience that all who are called upon to introduce a speaker appreciate a list of the speaker's qualifications and, for that matter, the vast, vast majority don't mind being told what to say.

Do not take the introduction of you as the speaker lightly. Done correctly, an introduction of the speaker can greatly enhance the effectiveness of the speech. Conversely, if done poorly, it can make being effective more difficult. The introduction of the speaker is like wrapping a Christmas present. A gift handed to you in a paper sack would not arouse your interest nearly as much as one tastefully, thoughtfully, and beautifully wrapped.

Approach the Podium Confidently A speaker should walk calmly and confidently to the podium in such a way as to relax the audience and build confidence without appearing cocky. Do not speak until you are standing behind the podium. When you get to the podium, pause and look at the people before you say anything. The mark of a novice is speaking before getting to the podium.

Suppose you are nervous, either because you haven't spoken publicly very much, because of your subject, or because of the occasion. In that case, you can relieve some tension by breathing and relaxing as you stand behind the podium before you utter your first word. Those few fleeting seconds it takes for you to take a breath and let it out may seem like an eternity to you, but if not done so that the audience does not see it, that pause will project confidence. It will make you look like a confident professional instead of a clumsy amateur.

Sincerely Compliment the Audience On some occasions, such as a pastor speaking to his Sunday morning congregation, it may be appropriate to begin with the introduction to the speech without speaking personally to the audience about yourself or them. On the other hand, there are many occasions when such an approach would be inappropriate. On those occasions, speakers often begin by saying something about themselves or something complimentary about the audience. If you compliment the people: 1) Say it neatly—be specific and truthful. 2) Say it deeply—mean it. 3) Say it briefly—be short.

Use Humor Wisely Many speakers seem to think they must tell a joke before speaking. No doubt, humor can go a long way in relating an audience to a speaker and preparing them for what he is about to say. A good laugh is good medicine. Causing people to laugh communicates that you are a good person and we are having a good time.

That does not mean, contrary to what some speakers seem to think, that you must tell a joke before speaking. Nevertheless, if you use humor, make sure it is in good taste. Be brief. Do not overdo it. Beware of double meanings. Do not use sarcasm. Be very careful about whom you poke fun. Do not use ethnic jokes unless you are a member of the ethnic group. Ideally, if a speaker uses humor when he first gets up to speak, the humor should be related to the occasion or the subject of the speech.

Avoid Trite and Empty Remarks Worn-out and over-used introductory expressions such as "It's a joy for me to be here" or "I am happy to be back" come across to most American audiences as hollow.

Be Bent on Communicating Your Message While these preliminary techniques are helpful, do not get carried away with them. By this point, you should know well why you are there and what you are going to say. That message should be at the uppermost of your mind. Such an attitude again will subtly seep through your pores to the congregation. So, after whatever brief preliminary remarks you make are designed to relate the audience to you, move with purpose to the introduction, which is intended to relate the audience to your subject.

Methods of Relating the Audience to the Subject

A Russian proverb says, "It is the same with men as with donkeys: whoever would hold them fast must get a good grip on their ears!" (Robinson, p. 160). Introducing an effective message requires the audience to listen to a message on this subject.

More specifically, there are three things the introduction of the message should accomplish. All three directly or indirectly relate the audience to the subject.

Get Attention The first thing an introduction should do is get the audience's attention. Don't assume that just because you have a Bible in your hand and step behind a pulpit, the people in the pew will give you their attention. A few people in every congregation or class come to hear what the speaker has to say, but many, and perhaps most, have other things on their minds.

Therefore, the preacher or teacher must go after the minds of the hearers to force them to listen. This is so important that one homiletician has said, "If the preacher does not capture attention in the first thirty seconds, he may never gain it at all" (Robinson, p. 160).

Attention can be obtained through the first sentence, the first paragraph, or by presenting a problem that needs solving.

First sentence attention-getters include using a familiar quotation, a question, a captivating statement, or a paradox. A captivating statement may be a novel idea, a striking expression, or an old idea. At any rate, any number of opening sentences can be used to grab an audience by the ears. Here are some examples from my sermons.

Ask a rhetorical question.

Have you ever doubted that you have eternal life? Many have. In decades of ministry, I have probably counseled more people with that problem than any other ("The Assurance of Eternal Life," 1 John 5:6-13).

"Have you ever thought of having an affair? Have you ever been out of town in a motel and tempted to have a one-night stand? Or been on a date that was getting more and more physical?" ("Sex Is Not Sinful; It's Natural!" 1 Corinthians 6:12-20).

The speaker may rely on the first paragraph instead of just a single opening sentence. A story, narration, or illustration will accomplish this. The narration should include action that builds to a climax. In some cases, a biblical sermon could begin with the narration of the background material to get attention and introduce the sermon. Here is an illustration of an opening paragraph designed to get attention.

"God needs you! That's right. The statement is not backward. It's not that you need God; it is God needs you. Granted, an individual needs the Lord. He needs Him for forgiveness, fellowship, and fulfillment, but it is also true that God needs you. Let me clarify" ("God Needs You!" Nehemiah 11:1-3).

Here is a sample of beginning with a story.

In a small town north of Minneapolis, during a cold week in the winter, I taught the book of Galatians. One night after the service, a man who had faithfully attended and attentively listened to every message asked me a question. He said, "I know this may be an involved question, but why did God give the law?" ("Why Did God Give the Law?" Galatians 3:19-25).

Beginning with a problem the audience feels needs solving will also get their attention. Make sure that the message that follows genuinely speaks to the problem the introduction raises.

That's only the beginning. There are numerous ways to get the attention of the audience. The list of ways to begin a sermon is endless. Consider other ways to commence:

1. With a joke
2. With a quotation
3. With a definition
4. With a paradox
5. With a news item
6. With an object lesson
7. With a personal observation
8. With a parable
9. With a poem
10. With a cartoon

Create a Need The second thing an introduction should do is create interest in what follows. Creating interest is different than getting attention. A speaker could get an audience's attention by ringing a bell, but that alone would not interest them to continue to give him their attention. On the other hand, if a speaker genuinely created interest, he would automatically get people's attention.

Messages That Grab People By Their Ears

There is a difference between getting attention and creating a need. One of my homiletics teachers and my personal mentor was Dr. Haddon Robinson. I can remember, until this day, a homiletics class he taught in 1963 in which he illustrated the difference between getting attention and creating a need. He said it would be easy to get attention: all I would have to do is drop my pants. Creating a need is much more difficult. He lowered his voice and said, "If you listen to me for the next thirty minutes, I will tell you how to make a thousand dollars in the next thirty days." He added that if you create a need, you will get attention.

The people sitting before a preacher or teacher want to know, "Why do I need to listen to this?" To be effective, you must show them at the beginning that what you are about to say relates to them.

People have physiological needs, such as food, drink, sleep, elimination, recreation, and sexual expression. They have psychological needs, such as security, significance, self-worth, self-expression, and self-realization. They have sociological needs because they live with other people. These include the need to be loved and live harmoniously with others. People also need to know and understand. They have spiritual needs that include knowing God and walking with Him.

"Felt needs" is one of the catchphrases of our generation. People are more apt to listen to a speaker if they think he is about to help them meet one of their felt needs. The teacher of the Word must remember that, in the words of Dr. Dallas Willard, a former professor of philosophy at the University of Southern California, "Our deepest needs are often not felt."

How does a speaker create an audience's interest in listening to his subject? Simply announcing the subject could create interest provided, of course, that subject was of interest to the audience. If the audience's interest in the subject is in doubt, the speaker can create interest by showing the relevance of the subject.

By far and away, the most effective way to create interest is to touch a deeply felt personal need in the audience. Touching people's needs will get their attention and create an interest in what you have to say.

There are other techniques for creating interest. For example, vivid, creative word choice has a way of getting attention and creating an interest in a speaker and his speech.

Years ago, it occurred to me after I had studied a passage of Scripture and had its truth in my hand that what I possessed was the answer to a question or the solution to a problem. In other words, in deciding what the passage taught, I said to myself, "Here is an answer. What is the question? Here is a solution. What is the problem?"

I then put the question or the problem in the introduction to direct the congregation to the passage for the answer or solution. Regardless of how I begin, whether with a question, startling statement, a joke, a story, etc., between the introduction and the first point, I almost always insert the question or problem the passage will solve or answer. From that day to this, the single most common comment I receive concerning my preaching is that it is clear. Why not? I asked a question in the introduction and answered it by the time I concluded the sermon.

After practicing this technique for many years, I have concluded that asking a question in the introduction that will be answered by my message is a superb way of getting attention, creating interest in my subject, and introducing my subject.

Introduce the Subject. The third thing an introduction should do is introduce the subject. It should go without saying that an introduction should introduced, but unfortunately, thousands and perhaps millions of churchgoers each week are knee-deep or neck-deep into a sermon, and they are still asking the question, "What in the world is this man talking about?"

An effective message must at least introduce the subject of the message. It may do more. It may even reveal the whole idea or even the outline to follow, but it should at least introduce the topic of the message. The introduction of the subject or the idea should naturally flow and follow whatever else has been said in the introduction up to that point.

An introduction should not promise anymore or any less than the message will deliver. There are two dangers in the introduction. One is overkill and the other is under-kill. In overkill, speakers promise more than they deliver in the message. It is like digging the foundation for a skyscraper and building a chicken coop. "Sensational introductions to mediocre sermons resemble broken promises. When the preacher fails to meet the need he has raised, the congregation feels cheated" (Robinson, p. 165). In under-kill, speakers do not reveal their subject or where they are going.

Summary: Effective messages have introductions that relate the audience to the speaker and to the subject of the speech.

Robinson says, "An introduction needs to be long enough to capture attention, raise needs, and orient the audience to the subject, the idea, or the first point. Until that is done, the introduction is incomplete; after that, the introduction is too long. An old woman said of the Welsh preacher John Owen that he was so long spreading the table, she lost her appetite for the meal" (Robinson, p. 165).

In terms of time, an introduction should consist of about ten percent of the allotted speaking time, but however long the introduction or the complete message, "the first twenty-five words must seize attention" (Robinson, p. 161).

Chapter 10

Messages That Attract People

As I walked into the sanctuary on Sunday morning, I saw a lady sitting by herself, whom I had never seen before. When a lone visitor wanders into church on Sunday morning, I usually ask, "How did you find us?" After introducing myself and exchanging a few comments, I asked her how she happened to come to our church that morning.

She responded that she came because of the sermon title on the marquee in front of the church. I was preaching that morning on "How to Hear God Speak." When she saw the title, she said to herself, "That message is for me."

Messages have titles to attract people. When the title of a future message is put in the bulletin, on the marquee outside the church, in the newspaper, or announced on the radio, it alone could bring people to hear the message. Members may return. Strangers may appear.

Titles can also create a sense of expectancy. Knowing the title creates a sense of anticipation for people who were planning to come to the service anyway.

Of course, not all titles attract people or create expectancy. What kind of titles do the job?

The Principle

Anemic Titles Vague, general, abstract titles are weak. Refashion vague titles into something more specific. Recast general titles into the particular topics. Transform abstract titles by making them personal.

Attractive Titles The titles that attract people answer their questions, appeal to their interests, or apply to their needs. The most effective titles contain a *benefit* for the listener.

The Categories

Titles that contain a benefit can be divided into various categories. Reviewing these categories during title preparation will help probe possibilities.

The Subject Title Some titles announce the subject of the message. Such titles appeal to people already interested in the subject. Those interested in prophecy would be attracted by the title "The Pre-tribulation Rapture." Some subjects have a general appeal.

> "The Hard Times"
> "The Greatest Lesson in Life"
> "Maximum Joy"

A Statement Title A declarative statement can deliver a strong punch. For example:

> "You Can Marry the Wrong Person"
> "God Is After You"

A Question Title Nothing will stop people like a personal question if it is important to them. Questions arouse curiosity. Examples include:

> "Can Christians Lose Their Salvation?"
> "Is the U.S. in Prophecy?"
> "Is The Bible Reliable?"

How To Titles To begin a title with the words "How To" automatically conveys the impression that the message will be practical. Here are some samples.

> "How to Get Your Prayers Answered"
> "How to Be Happy—Though Married"
> "How to Prevent Conflict"
> "How to Handle Trials"

The Direct Address Title Titles can directly address the listener. They should leave out the word "you." These types of titles call attention to something about which people should think.

> "Beware of Being Sidetracked"
> "Arm Yourself"
> "Don't Settle for Second Best"

The Twist Title A new twist on an old expression will grab attention.

> "Don't Just Do Something—Stand There."
> "Insanity Can Be a Blessing"
> "God's Graffiti"
> "Don't Put Jesus First"

The Current Events Title Any title dealing with a current event will likely generate interest. Here are the titles I used when these topics were current events.

"The Now Generation"
"What Does Jesus Christ Think of *Jesus Christ Superstar?*"
"The Exorcist"
"Is There a Curse on the Kennedy Family?"
"The Bible and Y2K"
"Reflections on the Attack on America" (the Sunday after 9/11)
"Decoding *The Da Vinci Code*"

The Test

One way to come up with the most effective title is to write down several possibilities and, from the list, choose the best one. Test the title with these questions.

1. Does it fit the occasion?
2. Does it interest the group to which I will be speaking?
3. Would anyone come to hear this message based on the title?
4. Is it believable?
5. Does the title promise more than the message will deliver?

Summary: Effective messages have titles that attract people's attention.

Other categories exist, such as appealing to curiosity. It is also possible for the same passage, and even the same message, to have several different appealing titles. For example, the message of John 3 is that Jesus told Nicodemus he must be born again. Possible titles include:

> "The Testimony of A Jewish Senator"
> "The Teacher Who Failed His Own Course"
> "How to Start Life All Over Again"
> "You Can Have a New Beginning"
> "Goodness Is Not Good Enough"
> "How to Become a Child of God"
> "How to Become a Member of God's Family"

Chapter 11

Messages That Pack A Punch

When God spoke and the authors of Scripture wrote, they used words (1 Cor. 2:13). Any communicator should be concerned about words. Those who are communicating God's *Word*, of all people, should pay attention to their choice of words. Concerning expositors of God's Word, Robinson observes, "To affirm that the individual words of Scripture must be God-breathed and then to ignore his own choice of language smacks of gross inconsistency. His theology, if not his common sense, should tell him that ideas and words cannot be separated. Like jello, concepts assume the mold of words into which they are poured. As pigments define the artist's concept, so words capture and color the preacher's thought" (Robinson, pp. 175-176).

A speaker's choice of words is called style. Hence, everyone has style, whether precise, imprecise, boring, or interesting.

As Robinson has written, "There are bright words as bright as a tropic sunrise, and there are drab words as unattractive as an anemic woman. There are hard words that punch like a prizefighter and weak words as insipid as tea made with one dunk of a tea bag. There are pillow words that comfort people and steel-cold words that threaten them. Some words translate a listener, at least for an instant, close to the courts of God, and other words send him to the gutter. We live by words, love by words, pray with words, and die for words. Joseph Conrad exaggerated only slightly when he declared, 'Give me the right word in the right accent, and I will move the world!'" (Robinson, p. 177).

Francis Bacon wrote, "Writing makes an exact man in thought and in speech." Mark Twain said, "The difference between the right word and almost the right word is the difference between lightning and a lightning bug."

To produce messages that are exact and have the power of lightning, manuscript the message.

A Clear Style

The first objective of speaking is to deliver a clear message. Besides unity, order, and progression, the single greatest thing a speaker can do to ensure clarity is to use a clear style.

Simple Words A clear style consists of simple words. Unless a longer word is necessary, use a short word. Seventy to seventy-eight percent of the words used by such notables as Sinclair Lewis, Robert Louis Stevenson, and Charles Dickens have only one syllable (George G. Williams, quoted in Robinson, p. 183). "Seventy-three of the words in Psalm 23, 76 percent of the words in the Lord's prayer, and eighty of the words in First Corinthians 13 are one-syllable words" (Robinson, p. 183).

Short Sentences A clear style is characterized by short sentences. In the book *The Art of Plain Talk*, Rudolf Flesch contends that clarity increases as sentence length decreases. According to him, a clear writer will average about 17 or 18 words to a sentence and will not allow any sentence to wander over 30 words (Robinson, pp. 180-181).

Simple Sentence Structure A clear style contains simple, short sentences. As a rule, the sentence sequence should be subject, verb, and object. Each sentence should contain one thought. For two thoughts, use two sentences (Robinson, p. 181). Also, let the nouns and verbs carry the meaning. "Adjectives and adverbs clutter speech and keep company with weak words" (Robinson, p. 186). Use proverbs, that is, one-liners.

Repetition Repetition is another way to communicate clearly. E. V. Hill preached a message in which he repeated the word "hell" numerous times throughout the sermon. Another preacher kept repeating the sentence, "It's Friday, but Sunday is coming."

Restatement Restatement facilitates clarity. Restatement is different than repetition. Repetition repeats the same thing the same way. Restatement says the same thing in different words.

An Interesting Style

What makes a professor boring and a stand-up comedian interesting? Professors are boring because they speak in abstraction. Stand-ups are much more interesting because they speak in concretion.

Actually, interesting communicators of biblical truth move between abstraction and concretion, "climbing back and forth like a laborer on a ladder. To have meaning, particulars must be gathered up in generalizations, and abstractions must be taken down to particulars to be made understandable" (Robinson, p. 149).

Hayakawa puts it this way: "The interesting writer, informative speaker, the accurate thinker, and the sane individual operate on all levels of the abstraction ladder, moving quickly and gracefully in an orderly fashion from higher to lower, from lower to higher—

with minds as lithe and deft and beautiful as monkeys in a tree" (Hayakawa, quoted by Robinson, p. 149).

Be Abstract The Bible contains abstract truth. That being the case, an expositor of biblical truth will speak in abstraction. God is a Trinitarian Being. It does not get any more abstract than that! Even "husbands love your wives" is an abstract truth.

Be Concrete Communicate the abstract, but quickly move from abstraction to concretion, from general to specific, from principle to particulars, and from idea to illustration. Be specific.

Soren Kierkegaard complained that when he asked Georg Hegel, the philosopher, for directions to a street in Copenhagen, all he received was the map of Europe (Robinson, p. 149).

God is a Trinitarian Being. There is one God who exists in three persons. That is more specific, but even that needs an illustration. Husbands love your wives. Tell your wife you love her. "Say it with flowers. Say it with the dishrag, but whatever you do, say it with words" (Donald Gray Barnhouse).

An Imaginative Style

Research indicates that students in a classroom retain images they create while listening to stories better than information presented through reading or watching a video. The images they retain from stories are more expansive and more detailed. Therefore, speaking can be more powerful than television. When people watch television, they are watching what other people have imagined, but what they can visualize is always more exciting. Moreover, there are no limits on what you can imagine.

Paint Pictures Use words that paint pictures, that is, do not say more; let the audience see more. Use verbs and nouns that paint pictures. Use metaphors and similes. "Figures of speech conserve time by packing more into a phrase than a word-wasting speaker expresses in a paragraph" (Robinson, p. 187).

Appeal to the Senses People learn about the world through hearing, seeing, smell, taste, and touch. Hence, speakers should appeal to the five senses to get an audience to experience the message. "Language makes listeners recall impressions of past experiences and respond to the words as they did to the event" (Robinson, p. 185).

Talk about People Incarnate truth, that is, talk about people and human experience. The Bible does. It speaks of greedy Lot, cunning Jacob, moody Elijah, passionate David, treacherous Judas, impulsive Peter, and determined Paul. The Bible contains truth in statement form, but most of the Bible is about truth exhibited in human form.

Use Suspense "Effective sermons maintain a sense of tension—the feeling that something more must be said if the message is to be complete. When the tension goes, the sermon ends" (Robinson, p. 165).

In the final analysis, the ultimate objective of speaking is not just to inform people; it is to impact people. Facts inform. Imagination impacts.

> I want a sermon that moves me. So many sermons seem to intend little more than to fill my mind with information. Yet, I already know more than what I am living up to. Like most Christians, my belief outstrips my behavior. I need a sermon that can encourage me. I need a sermon that can motivate me not only to know but to be and do what I already know I need to be and do. In other words, I need a preacher who will speak with rhetorical power.

(Kenton C. Anderson, "Moving Sermons: Did this message have rhetorical power?").

Summary: Effective messages are seasoned with a wording style that is clear, interesting, and imaginative.

Go from general to specifics. In the specifics, paint pictures (similes and metaphors) and appeal to the senses.

Effective communicators are wordsmiths. They labor long to say it just right. Their investment pays rich dividends. "A word fitly spoken *is like* apples of gold in settings of silver" (Prov. 25:11).

One evening, the English poet John Keats was sitting in this study with his friend Leigh Hunt. Hunt read while Keats labored over a poem. At one point, Keats asked, "Hunt, what do you think of this? 'A beautiful thing is an unending joy.'"

Hunt replied, "Good, but not quite perfect."

After a few moments of silence, Keats asked, "How about this? 'A thing of beauty is an unending joy.'"

His friend responded, "Better, but still not quite right."

After another long silence, Keats asked, "What do you think of this? 'A thing of beauty is a joy forever.'"

"That," said Hunt, "will live as long as the English language is spoken!" (Robinson, p. 176).

Word choice is critical. It is hard work but well worth the effort. Listen to these examples. William Temple's definition of worship is, "To quicken the conscience by the holiness of God, to feed the mind that the truth of God, to purge the imagination by the beauty of God, to open up the heart to the love of God, to devote the will to the purpose of God" (cited by Hughes in *Acts: The Church Afire*, p. 349). In an interview, John Hagee, Pastor of the Cornerstone Church in San Antonio, Texas, said, "The last time we saw Jesus Christ in the Gospels, he is hanging in the shame on a Roman cross wearing a crown of thorns; his face is covered with blood as he sobs in total agony, 'My God, my God, why have you forsaken me?' In the book of Revelation, his face is shining as the noonday sun. His eyes are like flames of fire, his voice the sound of thunder, and on his head is a crown. He is the King of kings and Lord of lords. Revelation is the story of truth over deception and hope over despair. The book of Revelation, when we truly know it, is a thunderous applause of God's victory over the world, the flesh, and the devil" (quote in the *Los Angeles Times* February 2007).

When I was in seminary, I had two homiletics professors. One told me, "Mike, God has given you a gift for speaking. I have one piece of advice. I recommend that you manuscript your messages. It is the only way that you will develop as a preacher."

The second professor told me, "Mike, God has given you a gift for speaking. I have one piece of advice. Do not ever manuscript your messages. It will hinder the natural flow that you possess."

Being a young man and a bit lazy, I took the advice of the second professor. After graduating from seminary, I began traveling as an evangelist. I preached the same messages repeatedly. I soon got to the place where I felt like I was stuck in a rut. About that time, I read the book *The Preacher and His Preaching* by Martin Lloyd Jones. Jones recommends that preachers manuscript their messages. As a result of reading that book, I began to manuscript messages.

That was in the late 1960s. I have written out every message I have preached since, with a few exceptions. After decades of doing that, there is no doubt in my mind that it has improved my speaking like nothing else I can imagine. It has forced me to think through what I am going to say and how I am going to say it. Consequently, it has made me a more exact, clear, and, thus, a more effective communicator.

And, oh yes, there is the added benefit of having a record of all the work and hours I have put into each of those messages. Using one of them again takes a lot less preparation time.

One other word. As Robinson says, "The manuscript is not a preacher's final product. A sermon should not be read to the congregation. Reading kills the lively sense of communication. Neither should it be memorized. An audience senses when a speaker reads words from the wall of his mind. Let the preacher agonize with thought and words at his desk, and what is and what he writes will be internalized" (Robinson, p.178).

Chapter 12

Messages That Are Appealing

Preparing a message is one thing; delivering it is another. Preparing a sermon is like the nine months of development of the fetus in the womb. Preaching a sermon is like giving birth. That which has been conceived and growing comes alive to the outside world. "A sermon ineptly delivered arrives stillborn" (Robinson, p. 191).

The delivery of the message is either appealing, making people want to listen, or it is repelling, causing people not to want to listen. In fact, a poorly delivered message jeopardizes its effectiveness.

What can speakers do to make the message appealing?

The Setting

The setting for the delivery of the message is a factor in the effectiveness of the message.

Sound Everyone in the audience must be able to hear you. A small crowd does not require an amplification system, but a functional PA system is essential for a larger audience. Make sure everyone in the audience can hear you.

Sight People in the audience need to see the face of the speaker. The podium should be as close to the audience as possible.

Temperature If people are too cold or if they are too hot, it is more difficult for them to concentrate. The comfortable range of temperature is between 72 and 78 degrees. Below 72 is too cold. Above 78 is too hot. If the audience is made up predominately of elderly people, who tend to get cold easily, the temperature should be closer to 78 than 72.

The Speaker

Non-verbal Communication A speaker communicates before he opens his mouth and utters the first word. Some aspects of nonverbal communication were discussed in the chapter on introductions. Speakers should be dressed appropriately and approach the podium confidently.

That is only the beginning. The Scripture recognizes the power of nonverbal communication. "A worthless person, a wicked man, walks with a perverse mouth. He winks with his eyes, He shuffles his feet, He points with his fingers" (Prov. 6:12-13). The face, the fingers, and the feet communicate.

Albert Mehrabian, a psychologist, claims that only 7 percent of the impact of the speaker's message comes through words. According to him, 38 percent comes from voice, and 55 percent from facial expression (Robinson, p. 193).

So, it is not just our words that communicate; it is the tone of our voice, gestures, and body language. Robinson points out, "God designed the human body to move. If a congregation wants to look at the statue, they can go to a museum. Even there, however, the most impressive statues are those that appear alive. In most realms, the professional uses his whole body. The conductor of the symphony, a concert pianist, the baseball pitcher, the umpire, the actor, and the golfer all put their bodies into what they do. An accomplished speaker likewise lets his body speak for him" (Robinson, p. 198).

Do not be a talking head. Gesture. Make your gestures large and deliberate. Put your body into the gesture. A halfhearted gesture distracts rather than enhances the point.

Move. Bodily movement should enhance the message. Nervously pacing back and forth distracts the audience. A moving messenger captures the attention of the audience. Furthermore, the movement should be meaningful. Hamlet instructs his actors to "Suit the action to the word."

One way to communicate with the whole body is to stand in three different places on the platform as you make three brief points. People read from left to right. So, from the audience's point of view, stand to the left of the center as you make the first point. Position yourself in the middle of the platform to make the second point. Move to the right for the third point.

Make eye contact. Do not gaze over the audience's head, stare down at your notes, or look out the window. Look individuals in the audience in the eye. People mistrust anyone who avoids eye contact (Robinson, p. 202).

Verbal Communication Speakers emphasize what they say with variety in volume, pitch, and rate, including pauses.

God lowered His voice; He spoke in a still small voice (1 Kings 19:12). Peter raised his voice (Acts 2:14). "Emphasis comes through variety. Dropping the voice to a near whisper can put an idea into italics as effectively as a loud shout" (Robinson, p. 205).

A ministerial monotone puts people to sleep. Change the pitch of the voice. The master of pitch change was the veteran radio commentator Paul Harvey.

Change the rate of speech. At times, speak faster. Periodically, slow down. Slowing down can dramatically emphasize what is being said. Change the rate. By the way, most speakers need to speed up. James MacLachlan, a professor at New York University, says that faster talkers are generally more persuasive and more favorably regarded by an audience. He says slow talkers speak about 120 words per minute and fast talkers speak about 180 words per minute" (James MacLachlan, "What People Really Think of Fast Talkers" in *Psychology Today*).

Pause. Robinson points out that pauses are the punctuation marks of speech. They serve as commas, periods, and exclamation points. They are "thoughtful silences." He goes on to say, "A pause before the climax of a story increases suspense, and the dramatic pause introduced when a speaker feels deep emotion can communicate feeling more effectively than words. Pauses not motivated by thought or feeling, however, confuse a listener, just as random punctuation bewilders a reader" (Robinson, p. 206).

Summary: Effective messages are delivered by a speaker who communicates with body language and voice in a comfortable setting where the audience can see and hear the speaker.

Chapter 13
Conclusion

God says, "Preach the Word." To do that effectively, start with a sentence statement of biblical truth and then shape it into a message summary statement that fits your audience. After that, prepare the message with a beginning, middle, and end.

At the Democratic Convention in Boston (July 2004), Edward Kennedy gave a speech. After it was over, a TV commentator said that Kennedy had given a traditional speech with a beginning, middle, and end. She added that politicians today give speeches containing one-liners designed to get the audience to laugh or applaud and that she wished we could have more political speeches like the one Kennedy gave.

One-liners may be appropriate for sound bites; for a message delivered before a live audience to be effective, it will need a well-prepared beginning, middle, and end. To prepare biblical messages, follow these ten steps.

1. Discover the biblical Summary Statement.
   Messages that are biblical
2. Diagnose the audience.
   Messages that are effective
3. Decide on a message Summary Statement.
   Messages that are clear
4. Determine the development.
   Messages that people can follow

5. Designate the support material.
   Messages that keep people's attention
6. Develop the conclusion.
   Messages that move people's feet
7. Devise the introduction.
   Messages that grab people by the ears
8. Design the title.
   Messages that attract people
9. Draft the manuscript.
   Messages that pack a punch
10. Deliver the message.
    Messages that are appealing

You should learn all the methods of effective message preparation possible. You should follow all the sound advice you can get, but make sure you adapt it to yourself. You must be yourself. Phillips Brooks defined preaching as "truth poured through personality." Make sure God's truth comes through your personality.

As a class assignment in seminary, I interviewed W. A. Criswell, the famous pastor of the First Baptist Church in Dallas, Texas. During that interview, he told me, "Learn all the homiletics you can and then forget it."

Work at developing your speaking skills, but do not trust speaking techniques to do the trick. Trust the Lord to use His truth through you to change people's lives. It is important to learn all you can about speaking, but it is more important to let the truth of God burn in your bones and then open your mouth.

Conclusion

Summary: Effective expository preaching/teaching is the communication of a biblical concept derived from the contextual study of a passage and proclaimed with support material and application to today.

Do not do it because it is successful. Frankly, it's hard work. Do it because it is right. Preach the whole counsel of God.

Appendix: Peter's Sermon in Acts 2

The first Christian sermon was Peter's sermon in Acts 2. It has been called one of the greatest sermons ever preached (Hodges). It illustrates several important principles of preaching. Peter began with the audience. He expounds the Scripture (20 of 52 lines are Scripture). He applies the Scripture and he aims for a decision. There are only two or three personal pronouns in Peter's sermon.

Introduction

Peter begins his message by speaking to what they were thinking. Luke records, "But Peter, standing up with the eleven, raised his voice and said to them, 'Men of Judea and all who dwell in Jerusalem, let this be known to you, and heed my words'" (2:14). Peter addresses the crowd as "men of Judea," that is, Jews in Judea and as those who "dwell in Jerusalem," that is, foreign Jews (Alexander). Some mockingly said, "They are full of new wine" (2:13). Peter answered the accusation that they were drunk. He says, "For these are not drunk, as you suppose, since it is *only* the third hour of the day" (2:15). Peter charges they have made an accusation based on an assumption (see "as you suppose"). He claims they are not drunk because it is too early in the day; it was only the third hour, 9 a.m. Granted, it would be possible for people to be drunk that early in the morning, but Jews did not ordinarily eat that early, much less drink wine. Paul says, "For those who sleep, sleep at night, and those who get drunk are drunk at night" (1 Thess. 5:7).

Prophecy is Being Fulfilled

Peter explains that what they are witnessing is not intoxication but inspiration. He expounds the Scripture. He quotes Joel 2:28-32: "But this is what was spoken by the prophet Joel" (2:16).

God will Send His Spirit "And it shall come to pass in the last days, says God, That I will pour out of My Spirit on all flesh; Your sons and your daughters shall prophesy, Your young men shall see visions, Your old men shall dream dreams and on My menservants and on My maidservants I will pour out My Spirit in those days; and they shall prophesy" (2:17-18).

Joel prophesied that God would pour out His Spirit on all mankind, including both genders, all ages, and all ranks, not just prophets (Num. 11:29). Men and women, young and old, even servants will prophesy. They will dream dreams at night and see visions during the daytime. The coming of the Holy Spirit on all flesh explains men and women speaking in tongues.

God Will Show Signs "I will show wonders in heaven above and signs in the earth beneath: Blood and fire and vapor of smoke" (2:19). "The sun shall be turned into darkness, and the moon into blood, before the coming of the great and awesome day of the LORD" (2:20). Joel prophesied that God would show wonders and signs in heaven and earth. Wonders and signs are expressions for miracles. Wonders are miracles that cause awe and amazement and signs are miracles that point to a message. The miracles of which Joel speaks will occur before the Day of the Lord.

God Will Save "And it shall come to pass *that* whoever calls on the name of the LORD Shall be saved" (2:21). Joel prophesied that God would save those who called on His name. In Joel's day, a plague of locusts devastated the land of Judah. Joel saw the

Appendix: Peter's Sermon in Acts 2

plague of locusts as a type of divine judgment and he prophesied that God would "afterward" pour out His Spirit on all flesh. He predicted that the outpouring would be accompanied with wonders in heaven and on earth and usher in the great and terrible day of the Lord.

What exactly is Joel's prophecy, and how is Peter using it? Peter's use of Joel's prophecy contains two difficulties. The first is Joel says that his prophecy is for "the last days" (2:17) and that the supernatural signs he mentions would take place before the "awesome day of the Lord" (2:20). The second problem is the signs themselves. Are they to be taken literally or figuratively?

Peter says that what happened at Pentecost is what Joel predicted. Therefore, the outpouring of the Spirit predicted by Joel was fulfilled at Pentecost. The miraculous signs mentioned by Joel are literal and will be fulfilled just before the great and terrible Day of the Lord. Therefore, that part of the passage is still in the future. Peter quoted that portion of Joel to include the statement about calling on the name of the Lord. Marshall calls Pentecost the "beginning" of the fulfillment of the outpouring of the Spirit. There will be a complete fulfillment later before the great and terrible Day of the Lord.

Jesus is the Messiah

Peter transitions from Joel's prophecy to a discussion of Jesus at this point.

Jesus Worked Miracles "Men of Israel, hear these words: Jesus of Nazareth, a Man attested by God to you by miracles, wonders, and signs which God did through Him in your midst, as you yourselves also know" (2:22). Peter began addressing them as natives of Judea and professors of Judaism. Now, he appeals to the people of Jerusalem, not the visitors in the city. Peter points out that Jesus worked miracles and that they were well aware that He did because He did them in their midst. Those miracles, done by God through Jesus, demonstrated to them who He was.

Jesus Was Crucified "Him, being delivered by the determined purpose and foreknowledge of God, you have taken by lawless hands, have crucified, and put to death" (2:23). Even though Jesus worked miracles, He was crucified. Peter mentions two things concerning the crucifixion of Jesus. Christ's death was according to God's determined purpose and foreknowledge. The death of Christ did not take God by surprise. He determined beforehand that Jesus should die. Lawless hands carried out the death of Christ. Those with lawless hands are those without the law (1 Cor. 9:21), Gentiles. This is a reference to Pontius Pilate and the Roman soldiers. The foreknowledge of God did not relieve the human agents from their guilt in the death of Christ. Marshall says, "Here we have the paradox of divine predestination and human free will in its strongest form."

Jesus was Raised From The Dead "Whom God raised up, having loosed the pains of death, because it was not possible that He should be held by it" (2:24). When God gave Him up, they took Him up, but when they crucified Him, God raised Him. This is a favorite antithesis with Peter and repeatedly occurs in his discourses (see below on 3:14-15; 4:10; 5:30-31; 10:39-40).

"For David says concerning Him: 'I foresaw the LORD always before my face, For He is at my right hand, that I may not be shaken.'" (2:25) "Therefore my heart rejoiced, and my tongue was glad; Moreover my flesh also will rest in hope" (2:26) "For You will not leave my soul in Hades, nor will You allow Your Holy One to see corruption" (2:27) "You have made known to me

(2:28). Peter quotes Psalm 16:8-11. David spoke about his soul not being left in Hades and God's Holy One not seeing corruption.

The Greek word translated "Hades" means "the abode of Hades, the underworld" and in the New Testament, it is used for the abode of departed spirits (A-S). It is "the world of the spirits, the state of the soul separated from the body, without any reference to happiness or misery" (Alexander).

"Men *and* brethren, let *me* speak freely to you of the patriarch David, that he is both dead and buried, and his tomb is with us to this day" (2:29). Peter argues that David spoke of resurrection, but as they all knew, he died, was buried and his tomb was well known to the all. His tomb is mentioned in Nehemiah 3:16 and by Josephus (see Josephus, *Antiquity of the Jews* 7.393, 13.249, 16.179-83.)

"Therefore, being a prophet, and knowing that God had sworn with an oath to him that of the fruit of his body, according to the flesh, He would raise up the Christ to sit on his throne" (2:30). Peter also reminds them that David knew God had promised him that one of his descendants, the Messiah, would sit on his throne. This refers to the specific promise contained in 2 Samuel 7:12-16 and repeated in Psalm 89:3-4 and 132:11.

"He, foreseeing this, spoke concerning the resurrection of the Christ, that His soul was not left in Hades, nor did His flesh see corruption" (2:31). According to Peter, David was "consciously prophesying" the resurrection of the Messiah, and not that there was a deeper sense in David's words than he himself was aware (Marshall). He specifically points to the part of the passage that says that His soul would not be left in Hades, nor would His flesh see corruption (13:35-37).

"This Jesus God has raised up, of which we are all witnesses" (2:32). Having established from the Scripture that the Messiah would be raised from the dead, Peter boldly declares that Jesus is the one God resurrected. Furthermore, he says, we are all witnesses. "We" refers primarily to the twelve apostles (2:14).

Jesus Sent the Holy Spirit "Therefore being exalted to the right hand of God, and having received from the Father the promise of the Holy Spirit, He poured out this which you now see and hear" (2:33). Peter concludes ("therefore") that Jesus was not only resurrected, but He was also exalted to the right hand of God, where He poured out the Holy Spirit, which is what they see and hear. This was the promise by the Father (Jn. 16:7; 14:16).

"For David did not ascend into the heavens, but he says himself: 'The LORD said to my Lord, "Sit at My right hand" (2:34) "till I make Your enemies Your footstool"' (2:35). Peter explains ("for") the ascension of Christ by quoting Psalm 110:1. Jesus used this same Psalm of Himself (Mt. 24:41-46). Peter uses the same logic here as he did in expounding Psalm 16, namely, that what was said was not fulfilled by David. It could only be fulfilled by One who ascended into heaven and sat down to God's right hand. The "right hand" is a position of authority. Jesus received the promised gift of the Spirit by virtue of His exaltation, which He poured out upon His people.

Jesus is the Messiah "Therefore let all the house of Israel know assuredly that God has made this Jesus, whom you crucified, both Lord and Christ" (2:36). The conclusion ("therefore") of the whole sermon is that Israel is to know that the One they crucified was both Lord and Messiah. The word "Lord" is used in the highest sense, as the New Testament applies to Him passages in the Old Testament referring to Yahweh, such as Joel 2:32 (Bruce). It is used of God in this passage (2:39).

Appendix: Peter's Sermon in Acts 2

Summary: Believers on the Day of Pentecost were not drunk; they were experiencing the coming of the Holy Spirit, which demonstrates that the crucified, resurrected, and ascended Jesus is the Messiah.

In school, students focus on reading and writing skills, but we spend much more time in life speaking than we do reading and writing combined. People in their family life, individually with a friend and with co-workers in the corporate world, need to be able to communicate orally.

Bibliography

Barclay, William. *The Gospel of Matthew*, vol. 1. Philadelphia:The Westminster Press, 1958.

Broadus, John A. *On the Preparation and Delivery of Sermons.* Rev. ed. Edited by Jesse Burton Weatherspoon. New York: Harper, 1944.

Davis, H. Grady, *Design for Preaching.* Philadelphia: Muhlenberg, 1958.

Jowett, J. H. *The Preacher: His Life and Work.* New York: George H. Doran, 1912. Reprint. Grand Rapids: Baker, 1968.

Lybrand, Fred R. *Preaching on Your Feet.* Nashville: B & H Publishing Group, 2008.

Koller, Charles W. *How to Preach without Notes.* Grand Rapids: Baker. 1964.

Monroe, Alan H. *Principles and Types of Speech.* Chicago: Scott, Foreman and Company, 1955.

Robinson, Haddon W. *Biblical Preaching.* Grand Rapids: Baker Book House, 1980.

Rue, J. M., *Homiletics: A Manual of the Theory and Practice of Preaching.* Grand Rapids: Baker Book House, 1967.

Whitesell, Faris D. and Perry, Lloyd M. *Variety in Your Preaching.* Old Tappan, N. J.: 1954.

About The Author

G. Michael Cocoris is a gifted communicator. He can make even complicated subjects simple, clear, and practical. His breadth of experience has allowed him to relate to a wide range of audiences.

Michael received a Bachelor of Arts degree from Tennessee Temple University, a Master of Theology degree from Dallas Seminary, and a Doctorate of Divinity from Biola University. He traveled the United States for over a dozen years as a speaker. He has also been a seminary professor, visiting lecturer, and world traveler, including hosting tours to Israel and China.

Michael has pastored three churches, including a rural church when he was in seminary, an urban church, the historic Church of the Open Door, first in downtown Los Angeles and later in Glendora, California, and a suburban church, the Lindley Church in Tarzana California, a suburb of Los Angeles. While at the Church of Open Door, he had a daily radio broadcast.

Michael has written numerous magazine articles, mainly for *Biblical Research Monthly*. He has authored a number of books, including *Seventy Years on Hope Street, A History of the Church of the Open Door*; *The Spiritual Life, Clarifying the Confusion; Repentance, The Most Misunderstood Word in the Bible; Evangelism: A Biblical Approach; The Salvation Controversy; Lordship Salvation: Is It Biblical?; The Books of the Bible, the Subject, Structure, Situation, and Significant Verses of Each Book; Psalms, A Song for Every Situation, Each Summarized on One Page; and Counseling Theories: A Simple Explanation and Biblical Evaluation*. In addition, he was a contributor to The *NKJV Study Bible* and *Nelson's New Illustrated Bible Commentary*.

Michael is the pastor of the Lindley Church in Tarzana, California. He and his wife, Patricia, live in Santa Monica, California.

www.ingramcontent.com/pod-product-compliance
Lightning Source LLC
Chambersburg PA
CBHW070118080526
44586CB00013B/1326